I would like to acknowledge the Aboriginal and Torres Strait Islander people as the Traditional Custodians of the land on which I live and celebrate their knowledge and continued connection to sea, land, waterways, culture and community.

I would like to pay my respect to Elders past, present and emerging, both here on Wadawurrung Country where I live and to all First Nations peoples and clans across the country.

I would also like to acknowledge my ancestors who went before me and thank my family, friends, clients, colleagues and mentors who have contributed to my life.

The Mentally Fit Leader
Copyright © 2022 by Dr Julie Rowse.
All rights reserved.

Published by Grammar Factory Publishing, an imprint of MacMillan Company Limited.

Grammar Factory Publishing
MacMillan Company Limited
25 Telegram Mews, 39th Floor, Suite 3906
Toronto, Ontario, Canada
M5V 3Z1

www.grammarfactory.com

Rowse, Dr Julie.
The Mentally Fit Leader: Managing Your Own Mental Health to Improve Productivity and Performance / Dr Julie Rowse.

Paperback ISBN 978-1-98973-776-7
Hardcover ISBN 978-1-98973-778-1
eBook ISBN 978-1-98973-777-4
Audiobook ISBN 978-1-98973-779-8

   1. BUS071000 BUSINESS & ECONOMICS / Leadership. 2. HEA055000 HEALTH & FITNESS / Mental Health. 3. SEL024000 SELF-HELP / Self-Management / Stress Management.

Production Credits
Cover design by Designerbility
Interior layout design by Dania Zafar
Book production and editorial services by Grammar Factory Publishing

Grammar Factory's Carbon Neutral Publishing Commitment
Grammar Factory Publishing is proud to be neutralizing the carbon footprint of all printed copies of its authors' books printed by or ordered directly through Grammar Factory or its affiliated companies through the purchase of Gold Standard-Certified International Offsets.

Disclaimer
The material in this publication is of the nature of general comment only and does not represent professional advice. It is not intended to provide specific guidance for particular circumstances, and it should not be relied on as the basis for any decision to take action or not take action on any matter which it covers. Readers should obtain professional advice where appropriate, before making any such decision. To the maximum extent permitted by law, the author and publisher disclaim all responsibility and liability to any person, arising directly or indirectly from any person taking or not taking action based on the information in this publication.

THE MENTALLY FIT LEADER

Managing your own mental health to
improve productivity and performance

DR JULIE ROWSE

Testimonials

If you want to thrive as a leader, Dr Julie Rowse's book, *The Mentally Fit Leader*, is a must-read. It provides a clear roadmap for looking after your mental health and wellbeing. Drawing on her extensive experience and training, Julie has packaged up her immense wisdom into this easy-to-read and highly relatable book.

Michelle Bihary, people leadership and workplace resilience expert

The Mentally Fit Leader is a helpful resource to understand and apply strategies to live a more valued life. In her book, Julie has quite deftly been able to translate complex concepts into easily understandable and applicable strategies. This is a must-read book for all leaders looking for a better life balance.

Darren Gannon, Director & Principal Psychologist, InMind Solutions

Leading in our world is more complex and volatile than ever before. To intentionally move from surviving to flourishing, leaders need to be self-aware and prioritise their mental health and wellbeing. *The Mentally Fit Leader* is a practical tool to help you get started and make that journey a reality.

Karen Snibson, Principal, Phoenix P-12 Community College

Julie has always had a passion for mental health. Her book, *The Mentally Fit Leader*, comes at a time when society is finally emerging from the shadows and there is a willingness to talk about mental health, good and bad. The book is an easy read and offers everyday practical suggestions which are not hard for us to tend our own mental health needs. Let's face it, if we don't take care of our own mental health, how do we begin to look after others around us?

Des Hudson OAM. Chair,
Ballarat & District Suicide Awareness Network

Contents

About The Author

I am passionate about helping people achieve positive mental health so that they can lead rich and fulfilling lives.

I use relatable stories, metaphors and examples to help leaders understand their mental health and how they can optimise mental fitness to enable them to perform at their best. As a qualified mental health occupational therapist, speaker, coach and author, I work with businesses, organisations, schools and community groups to develop and implement positive mental health programs that will promote sustainable behaviours

I completed my PhD in 2011, and started Healthy Mind and Soul Pty Ltd in 2016. I've worked in public and private settings for over two decades and bring a wealth of knowledge and practice wisdom to the work that I do.

I love to share my knowledge to empower others and have given presentations at a variety of mental health conferences nationally and internationally – in Australia, Canada, the United States, Britain and New Zealand.

I live in regional Victoria, Australia. I value my mental health and often go bushwalking or to a day spa to help me to de-stress.

I believe it is through our leaders that we can improve the mental health and wellbeing of everyone in our world.

Introduction

Have you ever headed into your office, closed the door, sat quietly at your desk, and thought to yourself, 'Why aren't other people as dedicated to this company as I am?'

As you sit there pondering, you are aware of your level of exhaustion, which you have learnt to push to the side.

The long hours of work, the missed lunch breaks, the sleepless nights, the constant need of high-level energy to keep everyone's motivation up, including yours – all this effort can bring great reward, but it can also come at a huge cost.

As a leader, you work hard every day. You make sure you are available to the staff. You show how dedicated you are about the organisation, and others even comment on your level of motivation and enthusiasm. You have a clear vision that you share with all. You have a great elevator pitch and can speak about your organisation, comfortably, articulately, and with passion and conviction, without any preparation or forewarning. You would never ask others to do more than you would expect of yourself.

....

And yet, you are now wondering if this leadership
position was really worth all the hard work it took
you to get there.

....

Now, let's add in some external challenges – say, a global financial crisis, or a pandemic, which overnight can change the entire way you operate and do business. If your mental health is already at its limit, how can you stretch yourself to be able to adapt and survive massive challenges such as these?

But it's not just these once-in-a-lifetime events that we need to be able to manage. The world is a constantly changing and evolving place. Every year brings new technology, new government policy direction, new markets, new knowledge and skills, and new generations of people. We need to be able to adapt in order to thrive. This takes creative and strategic thinking combined with energy. These qualities become available if we are mentally healthy.

People who are stressed and run down have lower productivity, are less likely to meet targets, and are more likely to make mistakes, all of which can impact performance and profitability. The candle can only be burnt at both ends for so long.

As a leader, you are consciously aware of how important it is to confidently present yourself as the face of the organisation. This is not only for the benefit of those inside the organisation, to motivate them to perform at their best, but also for those outside the organisation, so they will connect and engage with your services.

....

Hence, your mental health impacts
your productivity and performance, and
sets the tone for how your workforce
looks after their wellbeing.

....

Here's the good news. Thankfully, learning to manage your mental health does not have to be difficult. Change is difficult, but the strategies known to promote positive mental health and wellbeing are in themselves simple and effective.

When you learn to manage your mental health you will feel better, and, in turn, you will perform better.

Think about it. When you come back from some time off and are properly rested – you have been active and eating well, have had some fun with friends – you have a spring in your step, your brain is pinging, and you are excited to get back into your work. We need to be like this every day, not just the first few weeks after a vacation.

This book will help you to understand what mental health and wellbeing is, and how to go about attaining it. It will explain why good mental health is something that everyone needs (including leaders!), and provide you with a plan for how you can manage your mental health and change your world at the same time.

When you are a leader, others will watch you and follow; you can change your whole company or organisation by putting your mental health first.

Too often, the responsibilities of leadership can cause us to overlook the need to address our own mental health and wellbeing. I know this, because I've been there too.

....

Leadership starts with looking after yourself.

....

Like so many others, the first leadership lessons I was taught by my businessman father were about work ethic, not about the importance of my mental health. People who succeed are the hard workers; a good day's pay for a good day's work. After many years of hard work and saving, my dad bought his first business. This is where I learnt the importance of not only hard work, but also strategic thinking – specifically, about how owning and growing a business generates more wealth than wages. My dad would build up a business until it was operating at its peak, sell it for a profit, and then move on to the next business.

As I progressed in my career I discovered that I, too, was driven to succeed, and ultimately found myself in senior leadership positions. By applying my dad's lessons of hard work and strategic thinking, I climbed the ladder and led teams.

However, my career was in mental health rather than retail businesses, and nearly two decades into that career I had to learn a new lesson. I learnt that my team *did* learn from me, in that they learnt to work hard, but didn't learn to look after themselves. Neither did I.

Physically and mentally exhausted, I left that job. I have since started my own successful business, and now live out everything I profess. I look after my mental health so that I can help other professionals, business owners and leaders to manage theirs so that they can succeed in their respective businesses, companies and organisations.

This is what I do on a daily basis, and in this book I've drawn on the lessons and learnings from my experience to help you.

I am a down-to-earth person, so this book is full of practical ideas and real-life stories that will help you discover what good mental health and wellbeing looks like, and how to obtain it.

So now I invite you to close the door, but instead of sitting with your head in your hands feeling stressed out and sorry for yourself, let's create some space for you to read so that you can start to implement some real, actionable changes in your life.

Ready?

How To Use This Book

This book is designed to be easy to read – ideally, it should feel like you are simply having a conversation with me. I wanted to capture the essence of what you as a leader need to know about your mental health, so that you can implement some simple and practical strategies in your everyday life that will be effective for you.

Let me start by clarifying what I mean by 'mental health'. I do not mean mental illness or mental health difficulties. When I use the term 'mental health' or 'mental health and wellbeing', I am referring to that state in which a person feels able to cope with and manage their emotions and behaviour in order to achieve in day-to-day life. It is a state of wellness, not illness.

Having worked in the mental health field for a number of decades, I am aware that a 'one-size-fits-all' approach does not get results. The key is understanding the principles of good mental health and wellbeing and applying them uniquely to yourself.

Learning new skills and making changes in life takes energy, and if you are already exhausted and stressed it can be incredibly difficult to find the drive to make massive changes. That's why, as you read this book and discover ideas on how to improve your mental health, you will notice that the techniques are all designed to be simple. Try not to over-complicate it! The simple things have huge benefits.

Part 1 of the book is all about understanding the cost of ignoring our mental health, and how the stress of leadership can impact our wellbeing. We will explore how investing in our own mental fitness can move us from surviving to thriving.

Part 2 will detail how we can build in specific actions, along with thinking and feeling strategies, to achieve good mental health and wellbeing. In this section you will learn about twelve practical concepts to improve your mental health, as well as strategies on how they can be incorporated into your daily life.

Part 3 will pull together the ideas and strategies we learnt in Part 2 into a plan – what I call a 'Mental Health Fire Plan'. After all, we don't achieve anything in life without a map to guide the way! Armed with our customised personal plan, we can not only change our own lives but also show the way to better mental health for those we lead.

Above all, have fun reading this book. I hope the stories and ideas in here are not only enjoyable, but also inspire you to become a truly mentally fit leader!

PART 1

WHY YOUR MENTAL HEALTH MATTERS

Are you thriving as a leader, or just surviving? Do you have the energy you need to get through each day? Are you overwhelmed by the stress and pressure of leading others?

When you are a leader, you are under numerous stressors and pressures. There is so much to be done: there are employees and customers to oversee and manage; changes beyond your control that can impact your strategic direction at any time; and tactical decisions that need to be made in order to progress and grow your organisation or company.

We can all take a certain amount of stress and pressure – indeed, as leaders, we can often take huge amounts of it. But eventually, our bodies will let us know that they can't take any more.

Have you, or someone you know, ever 'hit the wall', so to speak? When the stress is too much, our mental health and wellbeing suffers, and so too does our productivity and performance. We make more errors; our professional and personal relationships can be impacted; it may even cause our organisations to be less profitable, or fall short of our performance targets.

Everyone needs good mental health and wellbeing to function in life – yes, even you!

Having good mental health and wellbeing is a sound investment in yourself. This is exactly what we will examine in the first part of this book.

CHAPTER 1

Too costly to ignore

Do you remember when shops shut at lunch time on Saturday and were closed the rest of the weekend? Did you live in a time before mobile phones, when if you were out of the office people could only leave a message and wait for you to call them back? Can you imagine going back to a world where there was no computer, email or internet, and any information had to reach you by post?

That pre-digital world existed in my lifetime, and I still consider myself to be young! (Well, I guess technically middle-aged by now.) Advances in technology have occurred at a rapid rate over the past few decades, revolutionising the world as we know it. Being able to communicate instantly through telecommunication and internet services has made the world more connected than ever, and also created an environment in which we can work around the clock.

Have you received – or worse, sent – an email at 2am? I once worked with a CEO who would send emails in the middle of the night when he couldn't sleep. (Seriously!) Or are you someone who has notifications on so that if anything happens, day or night, you can respond? Technology has not only increased our hours of work, but also made our work so fast-paced that we sometimes have to struggle to keep up.

We cram more and more into our day. We travel more; we travel further. We do more tasks and activities. We connect more. We work more, and we work longer hours. And what does all this lead to? Stress.

The plain fact is that our bodies can only handle so much stress. Stress can come from situations that are both positive and negative in our lives. Getting married is very exciting but also stressful! Think about your mental health as a bucket into which you put all your daily stressors, worries and concerns, as Figure 1 shows.

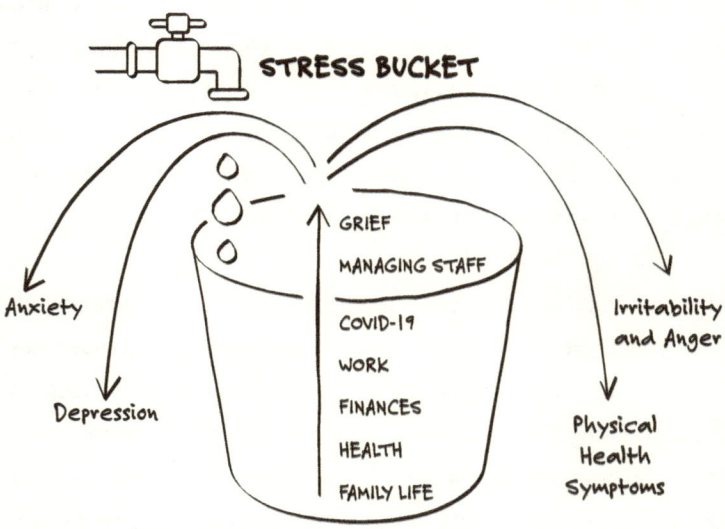

Figure 1: Your stress bucket

Some of us may have bigger buckets than others, but whatever size bucket we have, we are stuck with it. As stressors emerge in our life, the bucket starts to fill up. If we don't manage our bucket, it overflows. This means that our body has taken all the stress it can take, and something now has to give [1].

Some people experience this as fatigue or headaches; for others, their blood pressure goes up; some may experience a flare-up of other physical conditions. There are people who become more irritable and snappier, others who experience increased anxiety, and some who get overwhelmed and depressed.

....

When our stress bucket starts to overflow, our bodies let us know by showing signs of physical or mental health issues.

....

Urgent!

As a CEO, company director or senior leader, you will face myriad stressors on a daily basis. As more and more pressures present themselves – such as a global financial crisis; a pandemic; a significant change in technology, or political policy; a broken link in a supply chain; or a shift in consumer demands – your bucket could overflow.

An April 2021 article by Sophie Deutsch on the Australian HR Institute website indicates that CEOs are at twice the risk of mental health issues compared with the general population [2]. In an article from Horton International in May 2021, it was reported that 49% of CEOs admit to struggling with a mental health condition, and are also suffering from stress and fatigue [3].

....

The facts show that the pressure of being
the strong, composed and capable
public face of an organisation can be
tiring and stressful for a senior leader.

....

When we are stressed we do not sleep well, so we get increasingly tired. Tiredness leads to slower productivity. Tired and stressed people find it harder to think, and so their ability to generate solutions to problems is reduced.

I know that when I am tired, this is not the time to try and write a report or generate recommendations for a client. Firstly, when I am tired it takes hours longer to write a report than when I am rested, as I find it harder to think through and generate solutions. Worst of all, sometimes when I read through the report the next day before sending it off, some of the sentences don't even make sense!

When we feel overwhelmed by problems and difficulties, some of us try to cope by ducking the problem: avoiding doing things we find difficult, procrastinating, or even becoming work-avoidant by taking sick leave or time away, or simply by being unproductive at work. I've had clients who, when they knew they should have been focusing their attention on a planning document, have found themselves reorganising their office instead.

For other leaders, as the pressure builds they become more controlling to try and 'make it work'. Not only do they work harder, with the view that they are setting a good example for others, but they also demand that their people work harder as well. Or, they may start setting benchmarks that their workforce has to achieve, such as lower rates of sick leave or higher productivity targets. Adding even more stressors to an already stressful environment will only serve to increase employee sick-leave rates and lower overall productivity.

In fact, the World Health Organisation (WHO) estimates that stress and mental health difficulties cost the global economy US$1 trillion per year in lost productivity, while the American Psychological Association estimates that 550 million workdays are lost each year due to stress on the job [4].

Meanwhile, in Australia the direct economic costs of mental ill-health and suicide were estimated at $43–70 billion in 2018-19, which included an estimated $12–39 billion in lower participation and lost productivity. [5].

The statistics don't get any happier in Britain! Work-related stress and mental health issues cost British businesses an estimated £26 billion per annum, and account for over half of all work absences. Half a million people in the country suffer from work-related stress, and 57% of all UK employees report that they feel worn out by work [6]. Mental health issues are a major problem in the global workforce today. While a leader's personal stress may not necessarily be greater than anybody else's, because of their position it can amplify the collective stress of those whom they're leading.

....

The more stress and pressure on a leader, the greater the cost for the entire workforce.

....

So, what to do about this?

Build your personal mental fitness

Mental health is defined by the WHO as 'a state of wellbeing in which the individual realises his or her own abilities, can cope with the normal stresses of life, can work productively and fruitfully, and is able to make a contribution to his or her community.'

In the last several years, leaders in many industries have been recognising the cost of stress and focusing more and more on mental health and wellbeing in the workplace through educational programs and access to help – which is great! However, the importance of leaders being supported in their *own* mental health and wellbeing is a concept that has only recently begun to take hold.

....

Workplaces have become more aware of caring for employees' mental health, but the mental health and wellbeing of CEOs and senior leaders is often neglected – it's time for this to change.

....

In a 2019 article titled 'Why good mental health is a leader's best friend', Ben Brearley highlights the important role a leader plays in the overall mental fitness of a workplace. He explains that when leaders safeguard their own mental health they are better able to show empathy, which helps build rapport, trust and credibility within their teams [7]. Mentally fit leaders are also more perceptive, more able to adapt their approach when needed, and can keep showing up each day without burning out.

So how come it is often so difficult for leaders to achieve this?

We leaders, just like everyone else, have probably learnt somewhere along the line about the need to look after our physical health; however, we haven't really been taught how to take care of our mental health.

Whether we learnt it the hard way after having a bit of a health scare, or still remember the 'healthy eating pyramid' from our school days, we know that our bodies function better and are less likely to get sick if we eat a healthy diet and get regular exercise. But what do we need to make our minds function better? Remember any 'healthy thinking pyramids' for that? I'm guessing not.

While mental health and wellbeing has now become a far more central part of education and is included in school curricula, it was not routinely taught in the past. The fact is that most of us in the workforce today have not really considered the importance of addressing our mental health in the same way we do our physical health.

This principle applies as much to those who seem to have 'figured it out' as it does to everyone else. A 2019 article by Daniel Brooker in *Forbes* calls attention to how public figures and leaders may well be high-functioning, yet still capable of suffering from stress and anxiety[8]. This has implications not only for themselves, but also for their entire organisation. After all, people look to their leader for direction. In an emergency, if a leader can think carefully and communicate what is required articulately and effectively, this helps others to remain calm and know what they should do.

Hence, if as a leader you understand and value the importance of your mental health and are willing to learn about and embed mental health and wellbeing practices into your life, you will be able to manage the stressors you face, be productive, perform in your leadership role, and lead your team to do the same.

....

It's time to value your own mental health!

....

Productivity, performance, profit

Learning to manage your mental health is not dissimilar to learning to manage your physical health. Once you learn about and understand the important activities you can do that promote better mental health and wellbeing, you can start incorporating them into your everyday routine. Think about how you make a point to climb the stairs to your office in the morning instead of taking the elevator, or simply take a quick stroll in the middle of the day to stretch your legs – the same kinds of simple things you can do for your body, you can also do for your mind. You will be able to perform at your best when your mental health and wellbeing is in check.

Leaders with good mental health and wellbeing are more effective leaders, are more likely to empower their workforce to take care of their mental health, and therefore will have a more productive, higher-performing team and a more profitable organisation overall.

Sounds good, right?

In the next chapter, we'll look at what happens when you learn to prioritise yourself, and how this impacts everyone you influence.

SUPPORT FOR LEADERS

Research confirms that as people move into senior leadership roles, there is less support and investment in their mental health and wellbeing.

Bupa Global is an international company that provides health insurance to more than 31 million people worldwide, with the stated purpose of helping people live longer, happier and healthier lives. In 2018, the company conducted research with 1,556 senior decision-makers/managers in companies across the US, the UK, China and Mexico, and found that two-thirds of business leaders suffered from mental health conditions.

Despite the fact that 64% of these leaders reported that they were suffering from anxiety, stress and/or depression, one in four of them said that there was less support for mental health issues since taking on a more senior role. Even while the pressure of the role was increasing, the risk to senior leaders' mental health and wellbeing and the recognition of the need to mitigate that risk was less [9].

Even while there has been a great emphasis placed on reducing the stigma associated with mental health in recent years, 58% of the leaders surveyed in the BUPA study reported feeling it was harder to talk about their mental health and wellbeing in their position, due to fear that it would be perceived as negatively impacting their capability as a leader.

This study has encouraged and is continuing to encourage greater investment in support for the mental health and wellbeing of senior leaders, in addition to the workplace overall.

Mental health experts have commented on the benefits of senior leaders investing in their mental health, suggesting that by role-modelling mental health and wellbeing practices for staff they can assist in creating more mentally healthy workplace cultures overall.

It's time to invest in our most important assets – ourselves!

CHAPTER 2

Time to invest

Have you ever watched that 2006 movie *The Devil Wears Prada*? In it, Meryl Streep plays a ruthless magazine editor, Miranda Priestly, who takes on, as her new assistant, a young graduate and aspiring journalist, Andy (played by Anne Hathaway). The movie depicts a toxic workplace with excessively high expectations, a work pace that is frantic, and a work life that is all-consuming.

Hathaway's Andy is the character on whom most viewers focus their attention. While admiring her willingness to learn and grow in order to become successful in her job, we question her willingness to continue to extend herself and be so loyal to Miranda, an apparent tyrant of a boss. When Andy walks away from the job at the end of the film, we are relieved she is finally valuing her own wellbeing.

But let's take a moment now to look at Streep's Miranda. This is a woman who had to ensure the magazine was a bestseller – her job depended on it. To do so, she had to work long hours, to the detriment of her own personal life and relationships; not surprisingly, she expects the same of her staff.

When Andy is walking out on her job at the end of the movie, we see a momentary look of genuine puzzlement, even disbelief on Miranda's face, before she turns around and gets back to work. I can imagine she would be wondering why someone who had come so far and been such a fantastic worker would just leave it all behind. After all, in her eyes the cost to her own life that she's incurred by rising to the position of leader is simply the cost of success.

Do you really want this to be you?

As leaders, we know the importance of investing money and resources wisely to ensure optimal outcomes. We put time into our work and motivate our staff to do the same, so that our organisation is productive and performs well. We know that there is no growth without investment.

And yet, we are often so focused on investing in our company or organisation that we forget to invest in ourselves. Remember, *we* are our organisation's greatest resource, and if we break down, then our organisation's productivity suffers. If your company needs vehicles or machinery to be able to operate, you will ensure that those machines are serviced regularly so that the machinery lasts longer and performs at its best. The same principle applies to our own bodies and minds.

....

We must invest in our mental health and wellbeing so that we can continue to be productive and perform at our best.

....

Invest in you

Like Miranda in *The Devil Wears Prada*, those of us in leadership roles are normally strategic thinkers who can take a bird's-eye view and consider the bigger picture. We are perceptive and forward thinkers who can reliably predict how different approaches may impact our organisation. We are planners and implementers who make decisive investments that are targeted to meet performance goals. We are often high performers, and many of us thrive under pressure.

But we don't want to be a Miranda, who neglects her personal wellbeing in the name of running a successful business. At the end of the day, we are all human. Leaders need to sleep, just like everybody else. If we don't eat and drink properly to keep ourselves nourished, we won't function at our best; worse, our bodies can get rundown and sick.

No matter the example Miranda tries to set for her staff, there is no such thing as being a superhuman. We all have a breaking point!

Now let's consider Andy. Just like Miranda when she was starting out, Andy has high aspirations and is a hard worker. However, she learnt that when she stayed connected with her friendship group, they supported her and encouraged her, giving her motivation to go after her dreams. When she went out for a meal with close friends after a long day at work, it lifted her mood and made her smile. When she gave herself space, her creativity blossomed into success.

Take a minute to think about this, and the times when you yourself have adopted good mental health practices.

In my case, I have found that preparing myself for good mental health before getting down to an important task is not only beneficial, but also essential. Before sitting down for a three-day writing session on this book, I would go to the day spa and have a soak in the hydro pool and then have a massage. When reviewing our business plan, we can go on a retreat and connect with nature to clear our head so that we can then look strategically at how the business is going and consider its next directions.

....

Investing in your mental health can generate personal wellbeing as well as leadership success.

....

As we explored in the previous chapter, when leaders prioritise their mental health, they can create a more positive workplace for everyone. Emma Seppälä and Kim Cameron, in a 2015 article for the *Harvard Business Review*, present evidence that a positive workplace attracts employees, inspires greater staff loyalty to the leader and the organisation, and enhances both people's strengths and their ability to cope with stress. This leads to organisational achievements such as improved productivity, employee engagement, customer satisfaction and financial performance [10].

So, the question is, what do we need to do to get there?

Stop just surviving

First, let's take an honest look at where you are right now.

Are you working hard, burning the candle at both ends, putting out spot fires which pop up wherever you look? Do you feel like no matter how many hours you put in, you aren't getting anywhere? Do you focus on getting through one day at a time, or even just one hour at a time? If so, then you are just surviving.

Right now, you may feel you are thriving, but can you sustain it? Sometimes stress can sneak up on us and before we know it, we have 'hit the wall'. Do you get up in the morning with a bounce in your step and have energy for the whole day or is this a distant memory? (I'm guessing you had this feeling at some point, as people don't usually become leaders without at least a little get-up-and-go.) Are you in a place now where you feel like you can manage and sustain your current level of performance?

Take a look at Figure 2 below, and after considering thoughtfully for a few moments, put a dot where you think you are currently.

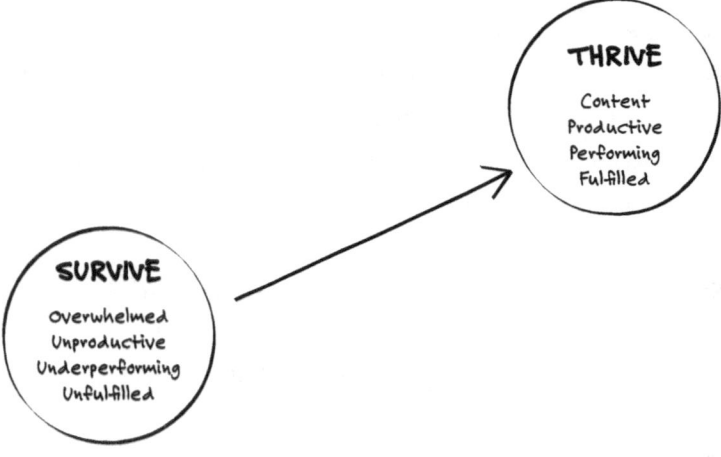

Figure 2: Surviving or thriving?

Surviving

If you are taking increasing amounts of time off work to try and cope with stress, or if you are at work but your inability to function is patently obvious to others around you, you are only surviving.

CEOs and senior leaders who are in survival mode will feel stressed and anxious. They may find themselves often feeling overwhelmed as their minds frantically go over their worries. Being consumed by this distress leads to lower productivity, as more time is taken up dealing with work stress than with actually doing the work. This, in turn, leads to low productivity and poor performance.

If you are in survival mode, you are likely experiencing difficulties sleeping (leaving you exhausted during the day) and your dietary intake will possibly be poor. You might have low motivation and be struggling to manage your emotions, which can make you more anxious, depressed and/or irritable. Your ability to think clearly and strategically will be affected.

What this all means, essentially, is that your 'stress bucket', which we discussed in Chapter 1, has filled up to the very top, and all that stress is now sloshing over the sides.

....

CEOs and senior leaders are high performing people and should not be content to just be 'surviving'.

....

Now take a moment to think back a bit. Have you ever experienced a time in your life when you felt like you were truly thriving in your job? Or maybe you have never experienced what thriving is like, but would like to?

Congratulations! Reading this book is the first step in helping you move beyond just surviving. Now is the time to learn what good mental health and wellbeing is, and what steps and strategies you can put into place to reach that state. In order to stop just surviving and start to thrive, you will need to begin engaging in daily mental health practices to improve your overall wellbeing.

Thriving

A thriving leader is mentally healthy, has a good level of productivity and is performing well in life. If you are a thriving leader, you have a sound basis on which you are managing your mental health and wellbeing. You have good daily patterns to ensure you get rest and feed your body to enable you to be productive. You have good problem-solving abilities and can manage your emotions to ensure clear and strategic thinking.

Even when under pressure, thriving leaders are psychologically flexible and able to manage even very intense emotions without losing their coolness and clarity. If you have successfully embedded mental health and wellbeing practices into your daily routine, you are likely to cope with times of crisis and maintain productivity and performance by being adaptable and able to capture opportunities.

Thriving leaders know how to manage their stress bucket. As Figure 3 shows, there are two ways to control the amount of stress in your bucket.

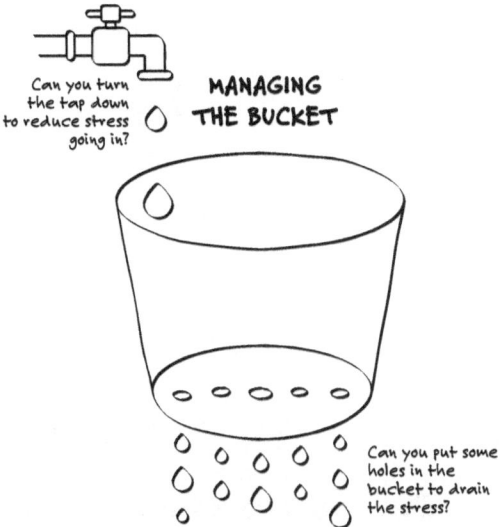

Can you turn the tap down to reduce stress going in?

MANAGING THE BUCKET

Can you put some holes in the bucket to drain the stress?

Figure 3: Managing your stress bucket

We can turn the tap down to reduce the stress flowing into our bucket by taking things out of the bucket, such as choosing not to take on further study or training during busy periods of work. If we can't remove a stressor from the bucket, we can reduce the impact by using our problem-solving skills. For example, the stress of managing finances may always be in the bucket, but if we effectively manage our budget the stress may not have to take up so much room in it (turning the tap down rather than off).

However, there are some stressors in our bucket that we can't take out or reduce the impact of. For example, we have no control over COVID-19 and its associated restrictions; we also don't get to choose when a family member or close friend may pass away. In cases like these, it's people who know how to drain out some of that stress by putting holes in their bucket who are able to keep thriving under pressure. Don't worry – this book is full of ways you can add those holes.

....

Thriving leaders are content with their life, are productive and performing, feel fulfilled, and benefit from having supports or structures in place to assist them in maintaining good mental health and wellbeing practices during high-pressure times.

....

So, stop and reflect: *Where are you now, and where would you like to be?*

Beyond expectations

Regardless of how stressed and 'just surviving' you may feel at present, there is hope.

I know that, as a leader, you naturally want to achieve at your work. Leaders are generally goal-orientated and highly motivated – that's why we work so hard and strive to improve everything we do.

The good news is that you don't have to sacrifice your goals in order to incorporate positive mental health and wellbeing practices into your life. In fact, when you are mentally fit, being able to achieve in your leadership role becomes much easier, because you will have more energy; you can focus; your thinking is clearer; your ability to problem-solve is improved; you can cope better with stress, and will be feeling more content.

Furthermore, if you as a leader prioritise your mental health and wellbeing, you will signal to others in your organisation that they too have permission to look after theirs. When they start doing that – when they make sure to take time away to rest and enjoy a holistic and fulfilling life in which work is just one component, not the be-all and end-all – the result is a productive work environment in which everyone is performing at their best. And that will be because you, as a leader, have enabled that balance through your example.

'Success' does not just mean being highly productive, exceeding performance targets, and maximising profits at all costs. In many cases, that is just the rise before the fall.

....

Success is managing your mental health
and wellbeing so you can not only sustain
productivity, performance and profit over time,
but also live the life you want.

....

In the chapters that follow, we'll look at how you can achieve that.

TAKE A CHANCE!

It can be hard to ask for help, especially when you are a leader. But let me tell you a story about someone who stepped out of their comfort zone and did just that. He was a tradesman who owned his own business – a family man who employed several other tradies and a few apprentices.

When we first met, he sat in my office clearly not knowing what to expect. He had come to see me because the stress of running his business was now impacting his home life, and his family had told him in no uncertain terms that it was time to get help. He was feeling so overwhelmed by the day-to-day pressures that by the weekend he was exhausted, his mood was flat, and he wasn't interested in doing activities with his family as he had in the past.

I drew the stress bucket up on the whiteboard, at which point he had an 'ah-ha' moment. He realised that he had just kept doing more and more to try and get ahead, and had never thought about looking after himself.

In the ensuing weeks, we worked through various ways in which he could turn down the tap and put holes in his bucket. We talked about how he kept all the company's jobs in his head and would verbally communicate information about them to his staff each day; a process that often resulted in a lot of questions. In our sessions, he was able to come up with a solution for this time-wasting exercise by setting up a workboard in his office that staff could refer to, thus helping reduce the constant questioning.

We discussed his frustration when deliveries were late, and were able to devise strategies that would help him focus on those things he could control. He also learnt the importance of getting to bed at a reasonable time and having a good night's sleep, so that his problem-solving abilities would be sharper at work. Within weeks, he was feeling better and performing more successfully in his role as leader. He was also back to enjoying time with his family on the weekend.

As you can see from this story, success as both a leader and a person starts with investing in YOU.

PART 2

HOW TO CREATE CHANGE

Thankfully, there are many well established strategies we can use to help promote good mental health and wellbeing. These are all centred on evidence-based behavioural therapy methods.

Near the end of the nineteenth century, the Russian physiologist Ivan Pavlov accidentally discovered that new behaviours could be learnt to replace old, potentially unhealthy behaviours. Noticing that the dogs in his laboratory would start salivating in anticipation of food when they simply saw the technician who normally fed them, he set up the famous experiment in which he would ring a bell whenever feeding the dogs. After a time, the dogs would start salivating whenever the bell rang, even if there was no food. Thus, the dogs had learnt a new behaviour.

Humans, however, don't just behave on cue based on such a simple stimulus as a bell. As we are far more complex beings, our thinking also helps determine the ways in which we behave. This led the American psychiatrist Aaron Beck to develop a model called cognitive behavioural therapy, which is based on the principle that our behaviour is intrinsically linked to our thoughts and beliefs. By finding ways to change those thoughts and beliefs that are unhelpful, Beck suggested, we will be better able to change our behaviour in order to achieve our goals.

Recent years have seen the emergence of a third wave of behavioural therapies, such as acceptance and commitment therapy or dialectical behaviour therapy, which factor in our emotional state as well. These models suggest that even if we have a clear action or goal we want to accomplish and have got our thinking aligned in the right way to promote that behaviour, we may still not be able to act as we want if we feel overwhelmed and fearful.

We're going to use what we know from these three 'waves' of behavioural therapy – the most effective and evidence-based treatments for mental health disorders available to us – to discover how we can proactively promote our mental health and wellbeing. This is about working smarter, not harder.

We're going to focus on three key areas:

1. Actions

Just as much as with our physical health, looking after our mental health is an *action*. We have to take decisive steps to properly look after our body. We need to get adequate amounts of rest to allow our body to repair and rejuvenate itself to face another day. We also need to get proper amounts of exercise: our bodies like to be active so that our muscles and brain get a workout and don't lose function. (You've probably heard the saying 'If you don't use it, you lose it'!) Likewise, having a routine of activities that promote mental health and wellbeing is key, and one that includes other people can help motivate us to engage in those positive activities.

2. Thoughts

To have good mental health, we also need to learn how to manage those pesky negative thoughts that can slip into our minds when we are under pressure – you know, the 'I'm-not-good-enough' type of thinking that can rock our confidence. It helps our mental health if we focus our energy on the things we can control in life, rather than allowing our mind to get consumed with things we can't change.

3. Feelings

We need to take notice of our feelings so we can keep them in check and use them to help us make decisions and connect with other people. Our feelings tell us so much, and can be invaluable in achieving our goals. For example, when I wake up and feel great, I am often motivated to go for a walk, during which I think of all I can achieve. However, if I wake up feeling tired and awful, I ditch the walk and instead spend my time having an argument in my mind about my capacity to achieve anything in the day ahead.

In the following chapters we will explore these areas further, and learn how to manage our actions, thoughts and feelings in order to attain good mental health and wellbeing.

CHAPTER 3

Actions

I once held the position of manager of a youth mental health team in a public psychiatric service. The team provided mental health assessment and treatment services for young people aged fifteen to twenty-four years across a geographical region of 48,000 square kilometres, with staff in four offices across the region. As the manager, I sat on the senior leadership team that held governance and operational responsibility for the mental health directorate.

The team was constantly busy managing a high volume of work. There were a large number of referrals, and our staff had heavy caseloads of clients to treat and care for. The work was high-pressure by nature, as many young people presented at times of crisis. This kind of emotionally heightened environment can take a toll on staff, so it probably wouldn't surprise you to learn that our team experienced a lot of stress.

As manager of the team, I wanted, and tried to encourage, staff to look after their mental health and wellbeing. I worked hard to support the team: I worked long hours and often skipped lunch; I made myself as available to them as I could; I travelled across the region to be present in all offices, so that everyone on the team could have access to my support and assistance. I advocated strongly for the team in higher-level meetings in order to maximise our funding and resources. I worked as efficiently and productively as possible, and I had a high work output.

My team got tired. I got tired. We had a high turnover of staff. (Sound familiar?) I was constantly recruiting and training. Meanwhile, as I was focused on working harder to make it better for the team, I didn't recognise how my relative neglect of my mental health and wellbeing was impacting the team.

Just like me, the team was working longer hours and many of its members were missing lunch, – there was just so much to do. They were tired and stressed from following my lead. While my intention in working so hard myself was to set a good example, I had instead led my team to neglect their own mental health and wellbeing.

Given that we were a mental health service, you would think that we, of all people, should have understood the importance of managing our mental health and wellbeing! But, when facing our heavy workload I, as leader, simply focused on trying to work harder, rather than ensuring that I was in the proper condition to help everyone to the best of my ability.

Think about when you're on an aircraft, and the flight attendants are going through the safety procedures before take-off. One of the key things they tell us is that if the oxygen masks descend from overhead, you should fit your own mask first before helping others. If we don't ensure we have oxygen ourselves, we may lose consciousness and then be unable to help anyone else. (Can you see where I'm going with this?)

As leader of the team, I needed to take action to prioritise my mental health and wellbeing so that I could motivate the team to take care of theirs: so that we could then help others as best we could.

....

As leaders, our actions set the tone
for our entire organisation.

....

No sleep if you're dead

As leaders, our everyday actions or behaviours are watched by those around us, and these let them know what is expected of them, giving implied permission for certain behaviours. If we say one thing yet do another, it is our actions rather than our words that send the stronger message.

When we are in leadership roles, it is all too easy for our time and attention to be directed to the big picture. We thrive on strategic thinking and troubleshooting issues so that our organisation can operate smoothly and be as effective as possible. With all this to worry about, it can feel a little odd to think about spending some of our valuable time planning and then embedding positive mental health activities, even such simple ones as taking an actual lunch break or going on a short walk, into the daily rhythm of our busy lives.

....

Yet it's the simple things that are often the best.

....

You might remember the above saying as the catchphrase for a Kellogg's Cornflakes ad back in the '80s, but it's true! Take eating breakfast as an example: this very basic, everyday habit gives our body the energy it needs to start the day, helps fuel our brain to be active and alert, and stokes our metabolism to help manage our appetite throughout the day. This is why we've often heard that 'breakfast is the most important meal of the day'.

Despite us knowing the enormous benefits of fundamental requirements such as dietary intake and sleep, through our actions we often implicitly demonstrate that we consider them to be minor and insignificant. But these basic activities have huge impacts on our lives.

I have heard some people say 'I'll sleep when I'm dead' to brush off their need to allocate hours for sleep. However, the Harvard Medical School advises that 'sleep deprivation affects your psychological state and mental health'. People with chronic sleep issues are more likely to have mental health difficulties such as anxiety, depression or mood disorders [11].

As far as I'm concerned, the importance of getting enough sleep comes even before that of having breakfast to start the day. It's generally the first thing I talk to my clients about when we're starting our work together. When you don't get the sleep you need, it impacts every aspect of your life. A properly rested body is in its fittest state, and has the energy it needs to move, think and engage in all manner of activities across the span of a day. By deprioritising sleep, you will hamper your ability to function and perform at the level you need to.

That crucial need for sleep feeds directly into another widely recommended daily activity: regular exercise. When we are active during the day, we sleep better at night. Our body benefits from being active, and the neurotransmitters in our brain fire off positive, feel-good energy that improves our mood. A happier and healthier you is a more productive and higher-performing you. Even something as simple and low-impact as a twenty-minute walk can have amazing effects on your outlook and the course of your day.

Then there is social connection, another thing we all need. Humans are relational beings – we enjoy shared experiences. Having friends and family with whom we can spend time, talk to about life, and participate with in enjoyable activities not only lifts our mood, but also helps us feel less alone. Surrounding yourself with the right circle of people can make a huge impact on your mental health and wellbeing .

It all sounds so simple, doesn't it? And yet so many of us forget to prioritise the basics. We are so focused on getting reports in on time or running to that important meeting that we wind up sacrificing lunch, a much-needed coffee break, or even sleep to meet the next work demand. Before we know it, our lives have become exclusively about dealing with the tough stuff, and there is no time to have fun with family and friends or participate in the hobbies, sports or leisure activities that we enjoy.

Having a work routine that ensures you are still getting enough sleep, eating regularly, being active and engaging with others socially is the key to good mental health and wellbeing.

Simple steps to change

Changing our habits is not easy. Even simple changes can be very difficult to implement, and when you start considering how this could affect the current pattern of your life, the prospect may seem daunting.

This is why I love the saying by the ancient Chinese philosopher Lao Tzu: 'A journey of a thousand miles begins with a single step.' When you're seeking to change your behaviour, it is best to first make one small adjustment and firmly embed it into your everyday routine; then make the next small adjustment, and then the next. One step at a time.

As leaders, we often want to see change happen quickly – instead of one step at a time, we want to take a big stride and cover three steps all at once. But when we try to make large changes in one go they can often be hard to sustain, and we end up reverting to our previous, familiar (and potentially unhealthy) habits. When you're setting out to change the patterns of your daily routine to improve your mental health and wellbeing, patience is key to making that change sustainable.

....

When considering ways of implementing good
mental health behaviours, think of how you could
apply these principles flexibly to your life in a way
that best suits you as an individual.

....

Below are four key areas for you to address in order to improve your
mental health and wellbeing. You may already do some of these
activities, which is great! There may also be some you used to do,
but as you got busier they dropped off; these may take you some time
to reintroduce into your daily life. You may also find that there are
some actions you have never tried, but that could prove to be valuable
for your mental health. So that even if you've never considered them
before, it might be worth giving them a go.

1. Look after your body

Let's start with sleep, which we've already established as crucial for
our ability to function properly and maintain good mental health
and wellbeing.

One of the principles of good sleep management is to have a regular
bedtime and wake-up time. I like to be in bed between 9pm and 10pm,
and my alarm is set for 7am (although I am often awake before it goes
off in the morning). I know others who are night owls and feel that
they are most effective in the evening, and so prefer to head to bed
closer to midnight and be up around 8am. There is no one perfect
time for us to go to bed and wake up, but if you establish a routine
that gives you a suitable number of hours of sleep, it will set your

circadian rhythm and your body will settle into a pattern (hence why my body wakes before the alarm!).

We also need time to wind down before going to bed – otherwise, we remain too alert and our bodies can't get into the relaxed state needed to go to sleep. There are a variety of ways to make sure our bodies are properly prepared for sleep. Some people stop having drinks with caffeine after lunch; others take a bath or shower before bed. Keeping technology out of the bedroom (all those illuminated screens!) is another tactic that is helpful for many people. For me, it's a night-time hot chocolate, sitting quietly, and maybe reading a chapter of a book that gets my eyelids drooping.

Another important principle is to make sure you are eating sufficiently and are properly hydrated. As we said above, fuelling your body with breakfast at the start of the day is the most important thing, but how you go about that can be a matter of personal preference. Some people like to go big with a full plate of bacon and eggs or a bowl of porridge; others may find that they feel weighed down when they eat too much too early, so may prefer a liquid breakfast such as a smoothie.

However you go about it, you need to make sure you're taking in the necessary amount of food. Food definitely impacts our mood: one of my favourite new words is 'hangry', which the Oxford Dictionary defines as 'bad-tempered or irritable as a result of hunger'. If you make sure you take regular meal breaks to give your body the nutrients it needs, you will not only have the energy required to do your work but also the capacity to properly manage your emotions in the workplace.

Our drinking habits also influence our behaviour. Caffeine can be a good way for many of us to feel like we are jumpstarting our day, but too much of it and we are buzzing – we can be frantic, easily distracted, and unable to properly apply ourselves to the work at hand. High caffeine intake can also contribute to anxiety: I once worked with a client who seemed to have terrible difficulty with anxiety, but after we talked about, and then implemented, a plan to cut down on coffee and energy drinks, those feelings significantly reduced.

On the flip side of a stimulant like caffeine is a depressant like alcohol. Some people like to take a drink at the end of the day as part of the winding-down process we discussed above, and going out for drinks with friends can be a great way of maintaining the social connections that we previously identified as crucial for good mental health and wellbeing. Alcohol may taste nice to drink but regular use of alcohol can lower our mood and motivation over time.

Another often-overlooked daily habit that can have great benefits for us is vitamin intake. Deficiencies of certain vitamins in our body can contribute to mental health difficulties. For example, low levels of folate have been linked to depression; lack of vitamin D has been associated with mood disorders; and people who are low in B12 can be prone to mood swings, irritability, and even paranoia. If you find that you are lacking energy and generally feeling flat, you may want to ask your doctor to check your blood levels – sometimes, just having enough of vitamins B and D in your system can noticeably improve your mood [12].

All of these are only a fraction of the many potential actions you can take to achieve better mental health and wellbeing – there are many more that you can explore on your own. But for the time being, let's start by prioritising one area where you can implement that first, simple adjustment in the process of you taking better care of your body.

Ask yourself:
- Is there anything you could do to improve your sleep?
- Do you need to prioritise making time for meals during your workday?
- Do you think you should see your doctor and have your vitamin levels checked if your sleeping and eating habits are healthy but you're still feeling flat?

Consider these areas, and then write down one simple step you can take right now to put yourself on a better track.

_____

_____

_____

_____

2. Be active

As already established above, being active and participating in some form of exercise is an important component of your mental health and wellbeing. In a 2006 article for *The Primary Care Companion to the Journal of Clinical Psychiatry*, licensed psychiatrists Ashish Sharma, Vishal Madaan and Frederick Petty firmly state that 'the health benefits from regular exercise should be emphasised and reinforced by every mental health professional' [13]. Among its many benefits, regular exercise can improve sleep, increase interest in sex, build better endurance, assist with stress relief, improve mood, increase energy and stamina, and enhance mental alertness.

This does not mean you need to rush out right now and join a gym! While some people love that kind of exercise, other people prefer playing team sports such as basketball or soccer, or engaging in more individual pursuits like tai chi or yoga. Your exercise preferences can also change over time: I used to love my spin cycle classes, but recently I'd rather go for a walk or a hike in the bush.

Think about how you can build being active into your existing routine. Even something as simple as parking your car a few blocks away from the office so that you can get a walk in at the start and end of your workday may help you feel better! Or, if you work in a high-rise building, you could choose to take the stairs sometimes rather than just hopping on the elevator. Even incidental exercise is a great way to get more active.

Ask yourself:
- What are some easy ways to incorporate incidental exercise into your workday?
- What more formal kind of exercise do you enjoy that you could add into your weekly routine?
- Do you prefer organised sport or something less high-impact, like a casual walk with friends?

Write down one way you will get active each week.

_____

_____

_____

_____

3. Have a routine

Routines help us transform a single positive action into a regular, healthy part of our lives. You can't just go for a run or hit the gym once and reap the benefits! When we make activities into routines, it requires less mental energy to perform them because we are no longer thinking about whether we *want* to do the activity, we are just doing it.

Morning routines are especially helpful, as they allow us to transition from a state of drowsiness and indecision to one of full alertness and readiness. Having a morning routine signals to your brain that it's time to get going, so it can simply get on with it and save valuable thinking energy for the workday. Do you lie in bed trying to decide whether you should get up now or later, and pondering whether you will eat or shower first? Or, like me, do you roll out of bed right into the shower, get dressed, have breakfast and head out the door? By the same token, the winding-down-before-bedtime strategies we discussed above signal to our body and brain that it's time to start shutting down for the day.

Of course, sometimes circumstances dictate that we need to adjust our daily routines or create new ones to deal with new situations. In addition to its more dramatic disruptions to our lives, the pandemic forced many of us to work from home, which had an impact on a lot of people's daily routines and, consequently, on their mental health. For many of us, the act of leaving our homes and going into a workplace is an automatic routine-setter, whereas when we work from home we need to consciously set that routine for ourselves. I had a client who figured out that she needed to put on a bra to be able to get into 'work mode', as working in pyjamas was causing a dip in productivity and thinking capacity.

A WebMD article from 2021, 'Psychological Benefits of Routines', stresses the importance of establishing both daily and weekly routines in order to achieve greater mental and overall health. A mentally healthy routine will have a good mix of personal care, domestic tasks, work activities, social connection, and fun and leisure activities [14].

Organising your daily and weekly routine doesn't just involve deciding what activities to do, but also at what time of day they should be done. Some clients I work with find they get weary as the day goes on, and can't keep their energy up; others have difficulty getting up and going, but by the end of the day are buzzing and at the peak of their performance.

It's thus often a case of grouping certain tasks within the time of day when we know we are best able to tackle them. For example, as I do my best thinking in the morning, I try to move my more cognitively challenging work to that time of day, and schedule my active but less mentally tasking chores to the afternoon. Those who aren't morning people, meanwhile, will likely be best off leaving their thinking tasks for later in the day.

Ask yourself:
- Which area of your life could use a little more routine?
- Do you need to set up a better morning routine to help you get going each day?
- Do you need to create a clearer work routine, or build some leisure activities into your week?

Write down an action you can take to start incorporating healthier routines into your day and week.

_____

_____

_____

_____

4. Be socially connected

As noted above, humans are relational beings. We all like to feel connected to others, but the ways in which we go about doing this can be different for each person. For example, are you a social butterfly who thrives on having a large group of people in your life, or do you prefer maintaining a small, intimate friendship group? You may also connect with people for religious or cultural reasons, or maybe family connections are important to you.

When it comes to mental health, there is no one right kind or amount of social connection required. It's all about the one that fits with your personal preferences. That said, it's often best that the people you surround yourself with share some key interests with you (this is typically what brings people together as friends in the first place), can keep confidences, know you well, and can encourage you.

Social connection can bring a needed element of fun and enjoyment into our lives. It can provide you with a space to talk about your hopes and dreams, as well as your fears and failures. Friends, family and loved ones can inspire you and help you find the courage to really have a go at your life goals; they're there to celebrate with you at times of success, and provide a safe place for you when things get tough.

According to PhD research by Eva Stubits, there is evidence that having a trusted person to vent to about your stress can help your mental health. Stubits compares the process of venting to lifting the lid on a pressure cooker to let out the steam: when we talk through our worries and stressors we can reduce our anxiety about them, allowing us to process the information, think more clearly about problems and, if needed, generate solutions to them [15].

As a leader, it is not appropriate to vent to your employees or people you may supervise or manage. However, there are many other options available to you, such as industry groups, business networks, personal coaching and mentoring, or a leadership group you are a part of. As a health professional, I find that having monthly supervision and coaching is invaluable for my own mental health, as well as having informal connections with other local health professionals in private business.

Ask yourself:
- Do you regularly make time to connect with others?
- Have you prioritised maintaining friendships and relationships? When was the last time you had a fun and enjoyable catch-up with your favourite people?
- Do you have a trusted person who understands you if you need to vent and let the lid off the pressure cooker?

Write down who you will connect with or keep connected with to help you attain and maintain good mental health and wellbeing.

_____

_____

_____

_____

Foundation for success

When building a house, we don't start with the roof, but with the foundation. Similarly, to be a successful leader we need a foundation of good mental health and wellbeing. That foundation starts with a set of simple, everyday actions and behaviours.

If you are getting a good night's sleep, then you will have the energy and motivation you need when at work. You will be able to think clearly and deal with difficulties as they arise. You will be able to manage your emotions properly, and will be less likely to be irritable or have a short fuse.

....

Having a routine in which mental health and wellbeing actions are part of a daily ritual makes your performance as a leader sustainable.

....

Don't waste precious energy and thinking time every morning waking up and wondering, 'How will I start my day?'; 'Will I take a walk first?'; 'Or maybe I should just shower and go to work?'; 'Will I have breakfast at home, or maybe get something on the way to work?' Having regular habits means you can save your brain power for the important things in your day.

As I mentioned earlier, my morning routine is pretty consistent: get up, go for a walk (if it's not raining!), shower, dress, eat breakfast, head to work. My getting-ready-for-bed routine has regular key elements too, including that all-important hot chocolate! By having a set routine at the beginning and end of the day, I not only conserve my energy for my important activities but also ensure that I perform those behaviours that I've found are good for my mental health and wellbeing.

We need to recognise that, as leaders, we are an important and valuable resource for our organisation, and just like any important resource we have to be properly cared for. If our organisation has a fleet of cars that help us provide services across a region, we need to make sure that we fuel them to travel the distance they need to go, and regularly service them so that they don't break down. If plant and equipment are crucial for our business, we have a regular schedule of inspection and maintenance so we can be sure that these resources are operating at their peak performance.

....

So, stop and check the tank on your mental health and wellbeing – where and when do you need to refuel?

....

ROYAL PROTOCOL

If you're looking for an example of people who live their lives through routines, one notable example would be the British royal family. In royal circles there are protocols for greetings, for the proper way to address persons of different ranks, for how cutlery should be placed on the table for a meal. But when it comes to their mental health and wellbeing, royalty has to engage in the same kind of simple practices that are available to the rest of us.

In a January 2022 article for *Glamour* Magazine, Fiona Ward wrote about Queen Elizabeth II's simple and effective sleep routine, which involves going to bed at the same time every night, sleeping for eight and a half hours, and then waking at the same time each day. Like many of us, the Queen also likes to read before bed, which is a great relaxation strategy to prepare one for a good night's sleep [16].

Other members of the royal family have their own effective sleep routines, such as avoiding caffeine in the afternoon by choosing a smoothie rather than a coffee. One royal credits regular yoga practice as the key to a sound night's sleep, and many others enjoy maintaining an active lifestyle (including the Queen, who likes a daily walk). After all, when we are active during the day, we sleep better at night.

A royal schedule is not for the faint of heart, so it only makes sense that the Queen would have to have fashioned strategies to care for her mental health given that she has reigned for some seventy years! Even though we may not be royalty, we, too, are leaders: having a good daily and weekly routine, including making sure we get a proper amount of sleep every night, is a necessity for all of us to maintain the mental health and wellbeing necessary to lead our own 'kingdoms'!

CHAPTER 4

Thoughts

'I can't run because my mum can't,' was my daughter's response to her coach at training one night. When she told me what she had said, my heart sank and my brain went into overdrive. I wanted to say to her that just because I can't run doesn't mean you can't! But I knew that wasn't going to cut it.

My daughter's story made me start to question some of my long-held beliefs about myself, including the idea that 'I can't run'. I decided I would learn to run to show my daughter that, if she put her mind to it, she could learn to do so too. But I was going to work on it quietly until I proved it to myself.

So, without breathing a word of my plan to anyone, when I headed out for my morning walk the next day I changed my usual amble into a slow jog. There is a lake near where we live that is six kilometres around, with markers every 500 metres. I decided that I would run between two markers, then walk between the next two, and so on until I completed the circuit of the lake. As the days went on, I progressed to running (well, jogging, to be honest!) for a kilometre, then walking for 500 metres. Then one day I just kept going, and finished the whole lake, running the entire time.

That night, when I excitedly told my daughter that I had run the whole lake, she was pleased for me but was resolute in her conviction that she couldn't run. So, I kept training, and was eventually able to run two laps of the lake. A friend and I then started to participate in running events: I completed the local six-kilometre run, followed by a twelve-kilometre run in a nearby national park, and ultimately worked my way up to a half marathon (twenty-one kilometres) at Uluru in the Northern Territory.

On that last race, I remember the slow jog I had adopted around the ten-kilometre mark, my feet pounding in the red dirt as I started to give in to exhaustion. A fellow competitor called out to me in support, and I responded that I was disheartened at my remarkably slow pace. 'You're not sitting on the couch,' was the reply. In an instant, my mindset changed. It was true what was said: I was in the race; I was having a go. In that moment, my mental mantra switched from 'You can't make it' to 'You can do this!'

That night at dinner, a fellow participant asked me how long I had been a runner. I quipped that I was certainly *not* a runner, to which he replied, 'But I saw you cross the finish line today.' It was true – I had indeed completed the whole twenty-one kilometres and crossed the finish line, and I have the medal to prove it. Even if I wasn't great at running, the fact was: I *could* run!

While my own running days have slipped through my fingers, my daughter can run now: she is actively involved in sport, and runs regularly for exercise and fitness. Both of us, at different points in our lives, had changed our 'I can't' into 'I can'.

....

How we think affects what we can do.

....

When the world shut down in 2020 due to the pandemic, did you think 'We won't work out how to get through this'? Or, when you were faced with having to adapt your organisation to new, advanced technology, did you think to yourself, 'I can't learn to use computers'? These are the same kinds of thoughts I used to have about my ability to run. When my thoughts were firmly planted in 'I can't run', I couldn't and didn't run. But when my thinking changed, so did my behaviour, and through that I was able to learn a new skill.

The same principle applies in leadership. When we think we can't succeed, then we won't. But when our thinking is positive and constructive, we can accomplish amazing things. (I'll say it one more time, proudly: I ran twenty-one kilometres at Uluru!)

Our brain is constantly making decisions, even when we don't notice. Doing nothing is a choice. What we eat for breakfast is a choice. How we think about ourselves, others around us, our situation, or our workplace are choices. Given that a choice is an *action*, imagine what you could do if you consciously harnessed the power of all those thousands of choices you make every single day?

Think of the old adage: 'If you realised how powerful your thoughts are, you would never think a negative thought.'

....

If you find yourself focusing on what you can't do, can only see the negatives in a situation, are struggling to think and make an everyday decision, consider this a warning sign that you need to do something about your mental health and wellbeing.

....

What lens are you looking through?

Our cognition acts much like a filter through which we view the world. We can compare it to wearing glasses. When a person who is far-sighted or short-sighted puts on prescription lenses, everything is brought into focus and can be seen clearly – this is much like the clarifying effects of venting that we discussed in the previous chapter. When you wear sunglasses, it turns everything you see darker – this is akin to the negative cast of our thoughts when we are feeling down or worried. Conversely, looking at everything in an overly optimistic light – you've heard of that old expression 'wearing rose-coloured glasses'? – is equally problematic, as we may underestimate problems or overlook potential risks.

How we perceive and understand what is going on around us is critical to being able to work with others, be productive and perform in our role, and solve difficulties when they arise. If we are not managing our thinking effectively so that we have a clear view that is free of negative filters, our mental health and wellbeing suffers.

Our cognitive skills are our greatest assets as leaders. Our capacity to think strategically, communicate effectively, and employ high-level problem-solving abilities is generally how we have found ourselves in CEO and senior leadership roles. Being able to take in and process large amounts of information and think tactically under pressure is the hallmark of a successful leader. We are the ones who set the direction for the organisation, and our people turn to us for strategic thinking when faced with challenge – whether it be a policy or technology change, or an extreme event such as a pandemic, a global financial crisis or a catastrophic weather event.

....

If we have not been looking after our mental health and wellbeing, negative cognitive filters can impact our high-level thinking and decision-making at potentially critical times.

....

The damage your thinking can do

At this point you may be asking yourself, 'Is negative thinking really all *that* bad? After all, many leaders are overthinkers, and this can serve them well by letting them pick up on potential risks early on.'

The answer is, yes: negative thinking can be bad for you! In fact, not only does negative thinking prevent you from having a clear picture of what is happening (which means you can't properly solve problems even if you recognise them in advance), but it can also actually harm your brain. Researchers at University College in London have found that repetitive negative thinking is linked to cognitive decline and problems with memory. This means that people who brood over the past and worry about the future can actually affect their brain's ability to think [17].

Long-term brain function aside, in the short term, the way we think has an impact on our leadership decisions – and this doesn't affect just us, but also the people who work with us, the people we employ, and the people to whom we provide services. Have you ever made a decision that has cost you? Maybe a decision to change the services you provided cost you customers. Equally, a strategic change in direction for your organisation, for example, deciding to change hours of operation impacting on shift times for staff, may have cost you one or more employees.

Sometimes, the effect of our decisions can negatively skew our perception of those who work for us. I have worked with leaders who thought their staff didn't care and weren't motivated. When we took away the cognitive filters and explored the facts of the situation, it turned out that their organisation was going through a change process. The staff, in fact, cared a lot about the organisation and believed strongly in how its services were being delivered – the reason that many members of staff appeared unmotivated was that they chose not to participate in new work processes, believing the old way was more effective. When it was recognised that the staff did care about the work, a conversation could be had about a shared vision of how to provide the best service possible.

When we as leaders are under stress and pressure to solve a problem, we can sometimes let unhelpful thoughts lead us to make hasty decisions – which, even though they seem likely to help resolve the immediate difficulty, can in fact create additional challenges for our workforce. This can lead to people becoming disgruntled, which increases their stress and can send them into a spiral, resulting in them taking more frequent sick leave or even leaving the organisation entirely. The more often this happens, the more *your* stress as leader will increase.

Managing your mental health and wellbeing so you can think clearly prevents these situations.

Reboot

Our brain is a remarkable organ. It is a living information processing system that operates our bodies so that we can perform a wide variety of tasks on any given day. The brain retrieves and interprets information from multiple sources – visual information from our eyes, auditory information through our ears, tactile information from our limbs and the skin all over our body, olfactory and taste sensations from our nose and mouth – and, based on that information, makes myriad decisions about the actions our body should take in response.

....

Much like a computer, however, our mental operating systems may sometimes need upgrading or adjustment in order for our brain to think and work at its best.

....

Have you ever felt like your brain is sluggish and not working at optimal speed? It might happen when you are tired or have a headache. On the other hand, you may have experienced times when your brain is in overdrive, with so many thoughts racing at once that you struggle to focus. Perhaps your mind is focused on an unhelpful cognitive filter, which can happen at times of stress and pressure.

Firstly, don't forget those mental health behaviours you learnt in the last chapter. If you are getting a good night's sleep, eating regularly so that your body and brain have the fuel they need, and have found a daily and weekly routine that works for you, then you are giving your brain a good chance of operating at a high level.

I have included a few other specific thinking strategies below to help keep your thinking brain working at its best. Before explaining each one, I want to remind you that even though learning new skills can feel clunky at first, it gets easier with practice. It's like learning to ride a bike: when we start we use training wheels, and we wobble all over the place trying to stay upright. As we get more balance and confidence, the training wheels come off, we fall over less frequently, and we can ride all by ourselves. So, if the techniques below don't come easily at first, don't worry – just keep working at it!

1. Reframe negative thoughts

Do you see the good in life, or can you be a wallower? Although having a positive attitude certainly helps promote mental health and wellbeing, as we know, life has its ups and downs. Our brain is wired to protect us: it looks out for potential risks and things to worry about so it can then switch into problem-solving mode to keep us safe. If we are not careful, however, we can become preoccupied with these worries, and our thinking can become negative and distorted. These unhelpful cognitive filters can impact our ability to think clearly and perceptively.

We all succumb to these unhelpful cognitive filters at times, particularly when we are under stress. It's important to learn how to manage unwanted thoughts so that they don't impair our decision-making and affect the way we relate to others.

....

To tackle an unhelpful cognitive filter, we first need to identify the thought, then determine if there is any evidence for it to be true, and finally generate a more helpful alternative thought in its place.

....

Let's take a look at a very common kind of unhelpful cognitive filter: 'Nobody likes me'. Those of us in senior leadership roles are often, of necessity, not included in many of the social aspects of the workplace, and at times our job can require us to have difficult conversations with people who report to us. This can create the belief in our minds that we are disliked by the people we work with.

Now, let's see if there is any evidence that this negative thought is true. Keep in mind, evidence is about *facts*, not feelings. You may *feel* that someone doesn't like you, but that doesn't necessarily make it the case.

An example of evidence would be a feedback form from a staff member stating that you are a horrible boss. But even though that is one concrete proof of your suspicion that 'nobody likes me', that negative judgment needs to be put into context. Perhaps one person doesn't like you, but look at all the counterevidence to the belief that *nobody* likes you: maybe you are happily married, have a group of friends with whom you catch up regularly, and the vast majority of your staff feedback forms indicate that people are happy in the workplace under your leadership.

Equipped with this evidence, we can now generate an alternate, more helpful thought. It might be something like, 'Not *everyone* likes me, but my group of people do'; or perhaps, 'The people who are most important to me like and care about me.' Whatever alternative thought you craft to replace your particular unhelpful cognitive filter, what's important is that it is a constructive one that can help you move forward instead of wallowing in feelings of insecurity and doubt.

It's truly remarkable how easy it can be for us to hold beliefs about ourselves that have no basis in fact whatsoever. I once worked with a client who felt they were not good enough for the job, but when we sat down and actually looked at the evidence – including the fact that the owner of the business had told my client that they didn't want them to leave and start their own business – it became clear that they were indeed a valuable employee, and were very much good enough in their job.

I've made some space below so you can think about any unhelpful cognitive filters you may have. Try looking for any supporting evidence for those thoughts, and then start generating alternative, helpful thoughts to take their place.

....

When you can identify and successfully manage
unhelpful cognitive filters your mental health and
wellbeing will improve, which will in turn help
you to think more clearly and with greater focus.

....

Let's have a try. Write down an unhelpful thought you have that
undermines your ability to perform:

_____

_____

_____

List any evidence you have that that thought is true:

_____

_____

_____

Follow that with evidence that the thought is *not* true:

_____

_____

_____

Finally, think about an alternative thought that would be more helpful:

_____

_____

_____

2. Focus on what is in your control

How often do you become frustrated with something that is outside your control? When we negatively fixate on things like the weather, government decisions, or the behaviour of other people, we can greatly increase our anxiety. As leaders, we are by definition trying to direct a larger or smaller group of people to act together in order to achieve our goals. Nevertheless, at the end of the day, the only person we truly have control over is ourself.

We are in control of what we say, what we do, and what we think – we do not get to control what other people say, do or think.

Think about it: even in the case of a parent and a child, the former can have *influence*, but not complete *control*. You can read a child a book, tuck them into bed, make sure the room is dark and comfortable, and kiss them goodnight, but you can't make them go to sleep.

But when we focus on what we can control rather than those things over which we have no control, we feel less anxious and frustrated and can think through how to best achieve our goals. For example, an event manager I was working with was very anxious about the registration numbers for an upcoming event, and was worried about how many people would actually turn up on the day. In our discussions, we focused on those elements of the event that *could* be controlled – things like the speakers who would be presenting, the set-up of the venue, and the catering.

When I met with the client after the event, it turned out that the day had not gone as smoothly as possible but, by focusing on those things that could be controlled, it had nevertheless been a success. They had ensured that all the speakers were engaging and dynamic; when the technology failed at one point, rather than panicking, they left it to the IT people to solve; not everyone who registered showed up, but the numbers were good enough and those who did come gave rave reviews.

Think of a time you were in a stressful situation recently. Ask yourself:

What was I in control of and what did I do to manage the situation?

_____

_____

_____

Was there anything I was focusing on that was out of my control, and which I should have let go?

_____

_____

_____

When you find yourself in a frustrating situation in the future, remember to have a think about whether you are trying to change something that is out of your control. Let go of what you can't change and focus on those aspects within your control which you *could* change in order to produce the most successful outcome possible.

3. Attitude of gratitude

The word 'gratitude' is making a comeback, and more and more research is showing the benefits it has for mental health. A 2021 article in *Harvard Health* detailed a study in which people in one group were asked to write down the things they were grateful for, while those in another group were asked to write down their irritations. After ten weeks, the members of the first group were feeling more optimistic and were even exercising more and going to the doctor less often, compared to those in the second group [18].

The study also explored the use of gratitude in the workplace, finding that managers who expressed gratitude to direct reports from their staff had a more productive and higher-performing workforce. For instance, in a team making fundraising calls that had been separated into two groups – one that received messages of gratitude from their manager, and one that did not – the staff members who were thanked by their manager made 50% more calls than those who did not.

In my case, I find it more helpful to focus on gratitude than simple positive thinking. When I'm feeling stressed and under pressure, I can still find comfort in those things I am grateful or thankful for, even though I may not be feeling positive at the moment. I can have a terrible day where nothing goes to plan, but I am still grateful for the glorious sunset that night.

Keeping a gratitude journal or writing down two things each day for which you are grateful can make a remarkable difference in your mindset. This has been a successful strategy for many of my clients, even if they have been doubtful at first. One client I was working with initially declared that he wouldn't be able to find two things he was grateful for all *week*, let alone each day. But he agreed to try it anyway, and when I next caught up with him the change in his demeanour was very apparent: he no longer looked sullen, and he even had a bit of a twinkle in his eye. Before I could even ask, he shared that not only had he been able to find two things to write down each day, but also on some days he had recorded three!

Do *you* have an attitude of gratitude? List some of the things you are grateful for below:

_____

_____

_____

_____

_____

Once you get in the habit of regularly reminding yourself of the things you are grateful for, you may be surprised at the general improvement you see in your mental health and wellbeing.

4. The art of problem-solving

I know that, as a leader, you already need to have exceptional problem-solving abilities. But I have worked with many clients who, when under stress, have forgotten to tap into that essential skill. What's funny about it is that sometimes when it came to the big, important decisions, their problem-solving was usually sharp and on point – it was when they were faced with more everyday things, interpersonal relationship decisions, or when under time pressure, that their skills were abandoned for a hasty, not-well-thought-out choice.

Problem-solving is a complex task that requires you to have the ability to, first, clearly determine what exactly is the problem, and then to consider as many solutions as possible with an open mind – that is, without any distorting cognitive filters. When examining possible solutions, it is best to first identify the benefits of each, followed by the potential drawbacks. Focusing on the good things first is a strategic choice.

....

Once our brain forms a negative viewpoint on an idea it makes it difficult to see the positives, so we may dismiss a potentially valuable solution if we look at the downside first.

....

However, it's after all the solutions have been explored and the best solution or combination of solutions has been selected that we can sometimes come unstuck – because even though we have decided on a solution, we don't always follow that up with a plan of how to implement it. For example, I've known of workplaces where the employees have agreed on sharing taking a lunch break so everyone can have time to eat, yet the plan never seems to get off the ground: no one has actually taken the time to organise the schedule to stagger the lunch breaks to keep work continuity. So, make sure that you always have a concrete set of next steps for implementing your chosen solution, or your good ideas will just evaporate!

The final stage of problem-solving is making sure you have instituted a schedule to review the progress of your proposed solution and check that it is working. If it has solved the problem, fantastic! If not, then you will have to take another tack – which doesn't mean abandoning your initial solution completely. Try reworking it first, rather than just giving up on it – after all, you selected it for a reason!

One tip I give to clients is to write down their problem-solving process, as it helps get thinking out of your head. Once it's down in black and white, you stop going around in circles in your mind, then the choice of the best solution becomes clearer, and you're better able to determine a plan to make it happen. Especially when done in a group setting, this helps everybody focus and feel like their contributions are being heard.

Let's see how this process plays out in a test case.

Think about a problem you have at your work at the moment. It may be best to start with something small:

_____

_____

_____

Brainstorm a few ways you could address that problem, and assess each one for its pros and cons.

POSSIBLE SOLUTIONS	BENEFITS/PROS	DRAWBACKS/CONS

Look over the list above and, taking each option's pros and cons into account, choose which solution or combination of solutions you think has the best chance of solving the problem:

_____

_____

_____

Think through how you're going to start putting your chosen solution into action:

_____

_____

_____

_____

_____

Establish when you will review your solution so you can see how your plan is coming along:

_____

_____

_____

Keeping a record of your problem solving enables you to review and track your progress.

Adapt to thrive

Leaders who can think broadly, clearly and strategically in order to determine the most effective solutions are invaluable to an organisation. Not only can they perform at a high level in their jobs, but they can also communicate better with those around them, which means healthier relationships in the workplace. With the higher level of morale and contentment that comes with that, you get higher levels of overall productivity, less staff turnover, and a workforce that is primed to perform. When you truly thrive as a leader, your workforce and your organisation thrive as well.

But leaders can only thrive if they are properly managing their mental health and wellbeing. It is not easy to learn and accept that you cannot control everything, but leaders who are able to do so are better able to care for both themselves, and their team.

....

Knowing how to recognise when we are under stress, correctly addressing our negative thinking, and focusing on what is within our control can help us keep our brain functioning well so that we can better set directions and solve problems.

....

THINK BIG

By 2018, the seven Harry Potter books had sold 500 million copies, been translated into eighty different languages, and been adapted into a series of blockbuster movies and a hugely successful stage production [19]. Yet this incredible cultural phenomenon may never have come to be if the series' creator, J.K. Rowling, hadn't firmly believed that her story was one that large numbers of people would want to read. What's even more incredible is that she believed this despite the fact that, at the time she came up with the idea to write her first novel, she was divorced, living in an apartment she could barely afford, and struggling to keep food on the table.

How did she maintain her faith in circumstances like these? In a speech at Harvard, she revealed her secret: 'I was set free because my greatest fear had been realised, and I was still alive.' With that newfound freedom, she set about creating her stories. After each rejection she received from a publishing house, she reaffirmed to herself that her story had value, and she tried again. Finally, after twelve rejections, her manuscript was accepted. And the rest, as they say, is history [20].

As leaders, we too are trying to make magic happen in our corner of the world. But nothing will happen if it is not first conceived in our minds. Thoughts are powerful: even when we are at rock bottom, the way we think can help determine our future.

CHAPTER 5

Feelings

Let's start this chapter by taking a look at three world leaders, each of whom came to prominence during some of the most crucial moments in their nation's history.

The first is Abraham Lincoln, the sixteenth president of the United States, who guided the Union to victory against the Confederacy in the American Civil War and issued the order that emancipated the enslaved peoples of the rebel South. Were you aware that not only at the height of the Union's setbacks during the war, but also throughout his life, he suffered from severe depression? Yet, even as he continued to struggle with his mental health, he never surrendered the power of positive thinking – in fact, he has been quoted as saying, 'Remember in the depth and even the agony of despondency, that very shortly you are to feel well again' [21].

Our second leader is John Curtin, Australia's fourteenth prime minister, who held the office from 1941 until his death in 1945 and successfully led his country through the most catastrophic years of World War II. Throughout this time, as former Labor PM Julia Gillard points out in an excerpt of a lecture printed in the *Guardian*, critics within his own party charged that he 'worried much about little things; he was afraid of people; he exaggerated difficulties: "He took losses as a personal responsibility and worried himself with an illogical feeling of individual blame"' [22]. Today, we would recognise these traits as anxiety, a condition that is experienced by many people in Australia and worldwide.

Gillard further details how even Winston Churchill, whom many credit for leading the UK to victory in World War II, during his first stint as prime minster, from 1940 to 1945, experienced repeated episodes of depression: 'Churchill could be so overwhelmed by depression he would spend days, even weeks, in bed, fatigued and disinterested, unable to concentrate. These dark periods happened multiple times over many decades,' she writes. Churchill referred to these spells as his 'black dog', and early on recognised the connection between this affliction and his ability to think clearly: in a letter to his wife in 1911, he notes that, '[My black dog] seems quite away from me now – it is such a relief. All the colours come back into the picture' [23].

So, if you are feeling stressed, anxious, down or a little flat, remember that you're in good company! Mental health doesn't discriminate: even great leaders have struggled with the same everyday but intense emotions that have confronted you. Having these feelings absolutely does not mean that you're unfit to be a leader. But what it *does* mean is that you need to learn how to cope with and manage these feelings in order to lead effectively. And unlike someone like Curtin, who lived at a time when a far greater stigma was attached to mental health struggles, you don't have to do this in silence and secrecy.

Leaders can show vulnerability by acknowledging their struggles with their negative emotions, while also showing others how to successfully control and manage their mental health and wellbeing.

We are emotional beings

If you are breathing, then you are also feeling and experiencing a range of emotions. Emotions are normal and natural. They're not good or bad – they just *are*. But at the same time, they also tell us things and help us to make decisions. For example, if we go for a walk and feel happy and content, those emotions let us know that walking is an enjoyable activity that makes us feel good, which motivates us to take more walks in the future. If a situation causes us to feel angry, it can alert us that an injustice may have been done, and we may choose to take action to right the wrong. When we feel lonely, this signals to us that we may be lacking in the social interaction we need, so we could then decide to get in touch with a friend or family member to organise a catch-up.

By the same token, when we feel nervous or anxious, this is our emotions telling us something – it's a warning sign for something potentially damaging to our health and wellbeing. These feelings alert us to risks, and give us the opportunity to make a choice to protect ourselves. When children are learning to cross the road, we *want* them to feel nervous when at the edge of the curb: this motivates them to look both ways and ensure there are no cars before they start walking.

When leaders start feeling uncomfortable, nervous or anxious in their role, the best thing they can do is to try and discover *why* they feel this way instead of trying to simply push it back down and keep going on as before. I have had several clients connect with me precisely because they noticed that their feelings were causing them difficulties in their roles. A partner in a firm once came to see me so that he could start to understand why he kept getting frustrated and irritated over small things, as this was impacting office morale. Another leader noticed feelings of anxiety following a critical incident, and was keen to learn more about how to cope with this while continuing to steer an equally anxious team.

Being able to recognise our emotions, understand what they may be telling us, and manage them helps us to problem-solve and make decisions. This is called emotional intelligence.

In a 2020 article for *Forbes*, Dan Hawkins cites multiple studies that show that emotional intelligence is twice as important for predicting executive performance than technical skills or IQ [24]. A strong emotional intelligence helps CEOs slow down their thoughts to stay calm, avoid impulsive or emotionally driven decisions, create more effective interactions, get more people involved and make more thoughtful decisions.

Recognise and accept

Sometimes, emotions can become so intense, overwhelming, persistent or pervasive that they start to impact our functioning. When this happens, we are at risk of becoming mentally unwell. In Australia, one person in five will experience a mental health difficulty in a given year, while 45% of us are likely to experience a mental disorder in our lifetime [25].

When a person's mood is down for weeks on end and has led to them having trouble with sleeping, eating, thinking, motivation and/or general interest in life, they may be diagnosed with depression. The WHO has identified depression as a leading cause of disability worldwide and a major contributor to the overall global burden of disease; in Australia alone, one person in sixteen is diagnosed with depression every year [26, 27].

However, the most common mental health condition in Australia is anxiety. Up to one-third of women and one-fifth of men will experience anxiety at some point during their lives [27]. Anxiety commonly induces physical symptoms such as a rapid heart rate, shallow breathing, sweating, shaking and fidgeting, in addition to cognitive symptoms such as worry and overthinking.

....

Learning to recognise signs of anxiety early on is key to being able to manage it.

....

As a leader, you have probably found that if a problem is brought to your attention early on it is much easier to manage than if it is left until later, or, worse yet, if it is hidden from you until it grows to such an extent that it requires significant time and attention to resolve. Managing emotions and mental health is exactly the same: the sooner you notice and identify what is happening with your feelings, the sooner you can do something about it.

Feelings can impact functioning

While we showed above how our emotions can help us with our decision-making, if we choose to ignore the warning signs our feelings are sending us we can find ourselves not only making poor decisions, but also potentially damaging our relationships with others.

When we are highly emotional, our thinking brain can give way to a sort of cognitive automatic pilot: words and actions will be unfiltered and unchecked as reflexive, primal instincts take over. This reaction, which is called the 'fight-flight-freeze-faint' response, is a survival mechanism that is embedded into our brains from the times when our species was more likely to be faced with frequent life-threating situations, such as an encounter with a hungry wild animal.

Although this might seem like a very unhelpful response, it is designed for survival: when faced with a shark attack, the Australian surfer Mick Fanning punched the shark in the nose, saving his life. Had the survival mechanism not kicked in, leading him to automatically punch, Mick may have been on his board, with his brain thinking and problem-solving, as he considered whether he should swim, stay or act. Meanwhile the shark could have bitten his leg off!

The thing is, even comparatively minor stressors can trigger that same response in us – and while that instinct may be helpful for survival in the wild, it's not so good for strategic business planning and successfully communicating with the people we need to help us attain our goals. When we are operating in a state of heightened emotions we are limiting our capacity to think clearly, solve problems, and steer our organisation in the right direction.

....

Given that, as a CEO or senior leader, you will almost certainly be under stress and pressure in your job, it is crucial that you develop your ability to manage your reactions to stressors and use your emotions effectively.

....

As noted above, as humans we are emotional beings, and our emotions don't leave us when we shift into 'work mode'. Think about the intoxicating feeling of falling in love, or the grief of losing someone close to you – powerful emotions like those accompany us to the boardroom, the factory floor, the business meeting, or to a performance discussion with an employee. As leaders, it is not only advisable but also necessary that we learn to harness these feelings so that they can help us in our work, not hinder us.

By reading, understanding and managing our emotions, we can use them to aid us in our decision-making and build healthy relationships in our workplaces. When you as a leader have taken the necessary steps to attain good mental health and wellbeing, you are more able to notice the positives in a situation and convey that positivity to others. Your energy and enthusiasm can fill a room, and bring your people along with you.

By contrast, if you are consumed with worry and frustration, your team can sense that tension in you, and be wary of connecting with you in the same way. Worse, you may turn your feelings outward upon the members of your team. You may be too quick to respond to questions or statements, and may not always react in a calm manner – you may be a little *too* direct, perhaps even harsh in your tone.

Let me give you an example of the latter situation. A business owner once came to see me during a period when his company was going through a merger. He was concerned because he had found himself snapping at his administrative assistant about minor matters in which she had not done anything particularly wrong, even though he was able to remain calm when faced with considerably more high-pressure situations. He was puzzled by these seemingly odd emotional outbursts, and didn't want them to damage his workplace relationships.

After discussing how our emotions and reflexive reactions work (as we did above), we were able to determine that it was in fact a *lack* of pressure that triggered my client's outbursts. When facing potentially stressful situations, he made sure to harness his emotions properly in order to remain calm, clear and reasonable; but when he was back at his desk in a more relaxed, familiar environment, he allowed that control to diminish to such an extent that even a minor irritation could lead to an angry flare-up. Once he understood what was happening, the client quickly took care to make sure that he was managing his emotions across all work settings.

Embrace your feelings

One of the dictionary definitions of 'embrace' is 'to accept willingly and enthusiastically'. Much like accepting a hug from a friend or loved one, we can be very willing to accept some feelings like happiness, contentment or enjoyment, but there are other, less appealing feelings that we are understandably not so keen to welcome. We need to realise that those feelings are not alien to us, but a *part* of us and to understand that all of our feelings can help us make the decisions we need to make as leaders.

Learning to properly embrace and manage our feelings is known as *emotional regulation*. When you are successful in this you will have better relationships, be more open to learning new things, be able to better solve the problems you encounter in your role, and will feel happier and more content with life overall.

Let's look at some of the strategies we can use to embrace our feelings and achieve emotional regulation.

1. Notice your feelings

Emotional regulation starts with paying attention to your feelings. Sounds simple enough, right? But you'd be surprised how difficult it can be for a lot of people to truly figure out what they're feeling at any given moment.

As a mental health professional, I frequently ask people how they feel, and while some can give me an answer without any trouble, others ponder for a bit before finally replying that they don't really know. Some people answer my question by telling me an *action* rather than a feeling – for example, 'I've given up.' But what is the *feeling* that has led them to 'give up'? Do they feel overwhelmed? Despondent? Hurt? Distressed? Are they just tired?

....

We can't learn to manage something we don't truly know about. So, we need to start with noticing our feelings so that we can figure out what they're telling us.

....

One way we can start noticing our feelings is by figuring out how they manifest themselves in our body. Can you feel your heart pounding as you prepare to walk to the podium to give your speech to the company? This is your body letting you know just how nervous you are. Do you feel as if you can barely sit still as you wait for the fantastic results from last quarter to be read out to the board? That's your excitement coursing out of you as a feeling of pure energy.

Let's give it a try:

Write down the feelings you are experiencing right now. (Remember, there may be more than one!)

_____

_____

_____

Now ask yourself: how did you go about identifying how you were feeling? What were the clues you picked up on, and how specific have you been in defining them?

If you struggled just now with putting your finger on how you're really feeling, don't worry – just keep practising this exercise each day until it starts coming easier.

2. Keep your brain working

Have you ever found yourself in a heated discussion or an argument with someone, only to discover after you've calmed down that you're not even sure what the argument was about in the first place? Or worse, did you realise that you were probably the one who was more in the wrong, and that the other person had actually made some good points?

Earlier, I explained how the thinking part of our brain can simply turn off in moments of heightened emotion, causing us to revert to our automatic responses. While this is very helpful for life-and-death situations, it's definitely not very productive when you're in the middle of a tense and stressful boardroom meeting, or having a difficult conversation with a colleague or employee.

The key to turning your thinking brain back on and keeping it on during these kind of stressful situations is lowering your heart rate by slowing your breathing. When we breathe in through our nose, pause a moment, then breathe out through our mouth long, slowly and smoothly, our heart rate will begin to slow back to normal and our thinking brain will start turning back on. It is now possible to think strategically, plan, problem-solve, communicate effectively, and focus on those things that are within your control.

Many of my clients tell me that this exercise is one of the best mental health tactics they learn from our time together. So, let's try it right now!

- Breathe in through your nose (like you are smelling that first hot, fresh cup of coffee in the morning).
- Pause for a second (and savour the smell).
- Purse your lips and slowly let the air out your mouth (as if you are blowing on your coffee to cool it down before taking a sip).

Do this for a couple of minutes, and you will feel your body getting calmer and your thoughts getting clearer.

3. Keep your feelings in check

Have you ever heard the phrase 'drowning in emotion'? People use this term for a reason. Have you ever stood in the ocean as a wave rises behind you, and then comes crashing down on your head? Our feelings can sometimes affect us in the same way. Or perhaps you feel more like you've been washed out to sea by your emotions, and are now bobbing around with no way to get back to shore.

We need to be able to experience our emotions without them becoming so heightened that our brain turns off. In the previous section I explained how controlled breathing regulates our heart rate and keeps our thinking brain on. In addition to this technique, we can also use sensory experiences to help keep our body calm.

For instance, if I notice that my emotional state is becoming agitated as I sit at my desk surrounded by dozens of sticky notes all calling for my attention, I take a short walk to the tearoom to make a peppermint tea. The smell of peppermint is calming for me, and the simple act of walking helps release some of the tension in my body. Likewise, after a long day in which I've been constantly engaging with people and putting my brain into overdrive, soaking in a hot bath relaxes my muscles and lets the stress drain out of me so that I can get a good night's sleep.

The trick is to find the calming sensory experience that works best for you. Some people I have worked with find it in going for a run, feeling the rhythmic and repetitive pounding of their feet coursing through their body. Others prefer olfactory experiences, like the smell of aromatherapy oils.

Sometimes, even just taking a bit of time to pay attention to our senses in the moment can take us from a place of feeling overwhelmed to one of calm and focus – we call this technique *grounding*. Notice what your body feels: your bottom sitting in the chair, the weight of your clothes on your shoulders, the texture of the pen in your hand. Notice what you see in front of you: the desk, the objects arranged upon it, the view out the window. Listen to the sound of the clock ticking, and the cheerful chatting outside your office door.

What helps you when you're seeking to manage your emotions? Write down some of the strategies that you use now, and think about others that you might like to try.

_____

_____

_____

4. Make use of your feelings

Once you have properly noticed, managed, and embraced your feelings, you can now put them to work for you. Two areas where you can really make use of your emotions are when you are trying to solve a problem, and when you are connecting with other people.

When attempting to solve a problem, we first need to gather as much information about it as possible – and our feelings can be sources of that information. For example, if you are feeling nervous or uncomfortable about something involving your work, this is your emotions letting you know that there may be some kind of risk here that you should be aware of and take into consideration.

Anger can be another useful warning sign. In the past year, a couple of people who are both leaders in their field came to talk to me about the feelings of anxiety and anger they had after going to see their doctor. In both cases, the doctor had told them that nothing was wrong with them, despite the fact that they were experiencing pain. Both of them were angry, feeling that they were not being heard by their doctor, and were still worried that something was wrong with them.

In each case, I talked the clients through their specific situation and reminded them that while feelings need to be managed, that doesn't mean they should be dismissed. We worked through the information available calmly and patiently, and determined that there was, in fact, good reason to still be worried. Armed with clear evidence, they each returned to the doctor and were able to receive the medical treatment they needed.

....

Keep your feelings in check, but don't dismiss them – they can be trying to tell you something.

....

Connecting with other people is another area that can benefit from you successfully using your feelings. Have you ever had a situation in which you had to talk to someone about a tough issue, saw that they were flustered and upset, and so decided to pick a different time to have the conversation? This is a case of you making a strategic social decision by using your empathy to read another person's emotions, and determining that speaking to them now would not be productive for either of you.

If our emotions can help us avoid potentially explosive situations, they can also allow us to bond with the people we work with. I remember the lunch we had to celebrate when our business had been operating for five years, and how the stories that various people recalled about our past successes helped strengthen our feelings of camaraderie and belonging. When people feel they belong in an organisation they are more motivated to contribute their skills to the overall direction of the team. But it's not just the happy times that bring us together: sharing our mutual feelings of frustration can be a powerful bonding experience as well.

Reflect on a time when you noticed a feeling in the workplace that motivated you towards an action that had a positive outcome.

_____

_____

Feel good and flourish

It would be great if we could be happy all the time, but this is simply not realistic. When we are in a leadership role we can experience a range of emotions on any given day, from the elation of success to the stress of an impending lockdown or the overwhelming pressure of a heavy workload.

When we properly notice our emotions and use them to make sound decisions and maintain healthy relationships, we feel good and can flourish as both an individual and a leader. We have an energy that drives us to be more productive, we use our time more effectively, our problem-solving abilities are enhanced, and our work output is higher because we can think and process information more quickly and be more targeted and specific in our goals. When we use our emotions to connect positively with others, we can better motivate our team and provide them with a model of how to get these same benefits for themselves.

....

Being able to experience a range of emotions and know you are able to manage them is a source of contentment, and thus of good mental health and wellbeing.

....

HARNESSING ANXIETY FOR SUCCESS

People often think of anxiety as something that prevents our ability to function; but while anxiety can indeed have this effect, it can also be a great driver for success. Often, a person who is a high achiever has risen to this level because their feelings of anxiety have given them the motivation, perfectionism, and attention to detail they need to realise their potential. Anxious people can be big thinkers.

This is why so many CEOs and senior leaders experience high levels of anxiety. But even though anxiety is one key to their success, if it is left unchecked and unmanaged it can lead to burnout and damaged relationships.

One leader I worked with initially dismissed my suggestion that she was experiencing anxiety, reasoning that her success and high level of accomplishment in her position proved that she wasn't being held back by these feelings. But the more we talked about it, the more she came to realise that things she had thought of as incidental or unimportant – her overthinking of every little thing, her excessive blaming of herself when she didn't meet her own extremely high expectations, and the irritability and quick-temperedness she exhibited at home – were signs that she was operating in a more or less constant state of anxiety.

Happily, this leader now understands what anxiety is and how to manage it, and now she not only continues to be successful in her work but has also achieved a quality of life that she never thought possible.

Anxiety can be a fantastic driving force for leaders, but even as it propels you forward to achieve your goals it can begin to undermine everything you were working so hard for in the first place. Effective leaders manage their anxiety to maximise their capacity for success.

PART 3

ADOPT SUSTAINABLE ACTIONS

Now that you have learnt about what good mental health and wellbeing is and strategies and techniques for achieving it, it's time to pull it all together into a plan. In the absence of a plan, nothing changes – the force of habit is strong, so without a clear set of goals and actions we can get sucked right back into old ways again.

To achieve optimum mental health and wellbeing we need good preparation, to know what to do when we are under stress, and to know where we can go for extra help if we need it. When we have these things clearly mapped out in a plan that's customised to our personality and preferences, we have all the tools we need. This doesn't mean that we won't still struggle with stressors at times, but we will know how to cope with them and continue to live a thriving life.

When we live a life that promotes good mental health and wellbeing, it can have a ripple effect on others in your sphere of influence. How you behave can have a powerful impact on those around you, whether it is your family, your friends or the people in your organisation – and when you're a leader, the effect on your workforce is amplified.

After all, people follow leaders, and to some extent model their own behaviour on them. If you demonstrate that you value your own mental health and visibly take actions that help you maintain it, just think of the possible benefits for your workforce as a whole.

It all starts with a plan.

CHAPTER 6

Plan to succeed

When you stepped into a leadership role for the first time, you had a vision of where you were heading or what you wanted to achieve – even if you didn't write it down in black and white, you had at the very least an outline of a plan.

Planning helps us become clear about where we are trying to get to and how we will go about getting there. When I decided to start a private practice, the first thing I did was write a business plan that articulated the whole vision for the business: its purpose, what it would aim for, the services it would provide, its costings, and a SWOT analysis that identified strengths, weaknesses, opportunities and threats. I did the same thing when I sat down to write this very book that you're reading: I wrote down why I was writing the book, who I was writing it for, what I wanted people to get out of it, and what each chapter should include.

(Well, to be honest, I actually started to write this book several times over the past few years – it wasn't until I connected with my amazing book coach and editor that I realised the reason I had kept getting stuck was because I hadn't started with a plan!)

Plans are crucial to so many professions. If you're a schoolteacher, you need to write down lesson plans to ensure that your students are covering all the necessary material in the curriculum. If you're a CEO, you need to have a business plan to ensure that your organisation remains viable and that you are steadily moving towards your business goals. Organisations also need contingency plans in case they need to adapt to new circumstances – we saw that in its most extreme case during the pandemic, when so many businesses had to radically change their way of operating.

....

> In the same way, you need to have a
> plan for your own mental health.

....

Don't just wing it

As leaders, we will know the importance of planning, setting goals and being accountable in our work life. We know how to use a Gantt chart, and we will likely be familiar with project management software and other tools that can help us devise and implement our plans. Yet, while we approach planning with a strategic mindset in a work context, we may be just winging it when it comes to managing our mental health and wellbeing.

For example, while I would never miss attending a scheduled meeting (except due to a family emergency), when it comes to going for a walk each day – which I know is good for both my physical and mental health – it can be easy to just let it slip. This is why it is so important to treat our good mental health actions the same way we would an important initiative at work – with a plan.

Luckily, planning is intrinsic to so many of the activities we engage in. Even those people who like to say that they 'take life as it comes' have an element of planning built in. For instance, when they set off on holiday and say they're just going to drive and see where the journey takes them, they still have a plan: they planned to go on holiday in the first place, and also planned that they would go about it in such a way that they would be able to stop and enjoy whatever they discovered on the way.

By the same token, people who obsessively plan out every aspect of their lives have to be able to adapt when things don't go precisely according to that plan. Maybe you are a planner: when you head off on a holiday the itinerary is well thought through, you have included everything you want to do, scheduled the timing of each event, planned rest times, researched the best places to eat.

But, despite our best planning, things can still go wrong or not turn out as we expected. The amazing holiday to Far North Queensland, with its white sandy beaches, suddenly ends as a cyclone moves across the ocean onto land, destroying everything in its path. Or you pitch the tent in a perfect location, sit down in the deck chair to relax, only to discover your child, who was happily exploring, has been bitten by a bee and suffers an allergic reaction needing medical attention.

If we don't plan at all we won't go anywhere.

We may desire to go on holiday but if we never get around to booking something and taking the time off, it will never happen. It is the same with our mental health and wellbeing; we may want good mental health, but if we don't plan and do something about it we will continue to remain stressed and overwhelmed. It is better to have some direction to work towards and tweak along the way than never start the journey at all.

Prepare! Act! Survive! Thrive!

Several years ago, I was asked to speak to a large group of high school students who were living away from home at boarding school. The school had identified that many of the students were struggling with mental health issues, and it wanted to be proactive in providing them with resources to deal with these problems.

These students mostly came from families who lived in rural areas, which meant that they were familiar with the fire plans that are necessary for Australians who live in regions that are prone to bushfires. Knowing this, I developed the concept of a Mental Health Fire Plan, which you can see in Figure 4 on the next page.

When we have a Mental Health Fire Plan, we have begun to lay the groundwork to achieve good mental health and wellbeing. When the stresses of life are raging around us, it gives us strategies to help us cope and a plan to rally extra support if we need it. While we can't control other people or situations that may arise in our life, we can choose how to control ourselves. We can choose how we think, how we manage our emotions, and the actions we take in life. When we

Figure 4: Mental Health Fire Plan

have a clear plan at the centre to take care of our mental health and wellbeing, we can move from surviving to thriving!

In the previous chapters we looked at a range of strategies and actions to help promote good mental health. Now, let's embed them into a solid plan.

1. Prepare

When preparing for a fire, we start long before the fire season begins. We ensure there is a clearance around the house as a buffer; branches and dry leaves are cleaned up, and gutters are cleared out. We check the water levels in our tanks and examine hoses and connections for deterioration, and either fix or replace faulty ones as needed.

In the same way, we need to prepare for when we are under stress so that we have effective daily activities in place that will help promote and maintain our mental health.

What mentally healthy actions are a part of your life? Do you have a regular bedtime? Are you going for a daily walk? If you've joined a yoga or tai chi group, are you attending it on a regular basis? Have you structured your workday for meal breaks to keep your body and mind working effectively? Are you making sure to stay connected with friends, family or loved ones?

What are you doing to ensure that your thinking is mentally healthy? Are you keeping a gratitude journal? Do you have an 'I-can-do-it' attitude as a part of your wellbeing approach? Are you making a conscious effort to focus on the things that are in your control, not those that are outside of it? Are you remembering to notice your feelings, and do you have regular activities you can use to keep them in check?

You will notice that I've been asking you questions, rather than giving you a 'ten-point plan for good mental health'. This is because we are all unique and individual in our likes, dislikes, strengths and preferences. You need to work out what works best for *you*. This may take a little trial and error on your part, but when you are clear on the cluster of actions and thinking and feeling strategies that best help you reach a state of good mental health and wellbeing, make sure to write them down. Then, at the end of this chapter, we will put them all together into one plan.

Prepare – what things will you do to promote your mental health?

Let's recall some of the positive things you do for your mental health that you identified and reflected on in Part 2, and write them in below.

Actions (e.g., take a lunch break, be in bed by a certain time, participate in a physical activity you enjoy, stay in contact with friends):

_____

_____

_____

Thinking (e.g., remind yourself what you are good at, keep a gratitude journal, focus on what you can control):

_____

_____

_____

Feelings (e.g., practise controlled breathing, notice your feelings, join a yoga class):

_____

_____

_____

2. Act

On an extreme fire danger day, those living in vulnerable areas need to take action to prepare for a possible fire. You connect the hoses to the water tanks so that they are ready for use; your overnight bag is packed and placed in the boot of the car; you regularly check local emergency channels so that you have as much warning as possible if a fire starts.

Our work life can also have high-risk days in which we are placed under additional stress and pressure. This is where our mental health plan needs to move past the 'be-prepared' phase and into proactive strategies for keeping our thinking and feelings in check.

We may need to make an extra effort to take breaks in the day and use them wisely to sit, slow our breathing, and focus on what we can control. We may need to write down our thoughts in a journal so that we can get them out of our heads and regain some clarity. Taking time before bed, we may listen to music and ponder what we are grateful for that day to help balance our negative thinking. Or, if more active pursuits are preferred, go for a run or to a gym class after work and sweat the stress out!

Ask yourself:
- When under stress and pressure, what works for you?
- What actions can you take to help you maintain your mental health and wellbeing when things are heating up?

Act – what do I find helpful when life gets stressful?

Actions (e.g., talk to a trusted friend, ensure you don't skip meals, choose an easier exercise to do so you can keep being active, get your vitamin levels checked by your doctor):

_____

_____

_____

Thinking (e.g., identify and address negative thoughts, let go of what is not in your control, write out your problem-solving method to help you think clearly):

_____

_____

_____

_____

Feelings (e.g., use your controlled breathing when stressed, go for a short walk at lunchtime, notice your feelings and use them to help your problem-solving):

_____

_____

_____

_____

3. Survive

It's a burning hot summer, what we feared has happened, and it is now crisis point – a fire has started. Immediately, you need to consider how close it is to you, how fast it is moving, and whether you should stay and fight or move somewhere out of danger. It is also important that you know what services or support are available to you if you do choose to stay, as well as community meeting points where food and shelter can be provided if you opt to leave.

Similarly, when we are under extreme stress we need to know where we can go for help. Do you have a family doctor you can speak with when the going gets rough? Are you aware of the different mental health support services in your area? Have you looked into online support options?

It's important that you take time to familiarise yourself with the support options available to you and have a think about who you would feel comfortable contacting if you need some extra help with your mental health. Write down their contact details on your plan so if you need them in a time of crisis, you already know whom you would prefer and how to access them.

Survive – when you need to press the help button, which person or service would you turn to? What are their contact details?

Name or service (e.g., family doctor, psychologist, Lifeline, online service):

_____

_____

_____

Contact details (phone number, email, website):

_____

_____

Mental Health Fire Plan

It's time to put all this information together into your own Mental Health Fire Plan. You can do this in the blank page included below.

Keep your plan somewhere you will always remember so that it's handy when or if you need it.

Below, you'll find an example of a Mental Health Fire Plan to give you some ideas as to what yours could look like.

MENTAL HEALTH
FIRE PLAN

PREPARE

What things will I do to promote and protect my mental health?

Actions – Set my alarm and get up by 7am each day, go for a walk after dinner each evening, have a hot chocolate before bed.

Thinking – Keep a gratitude journal and write down two things I am grateful for each day.

Feeling – Notice how I am feeling each day and take time out for a peppermint tea during breaks at work.

ACT

Strategies I find helpful when life gets stressful:

Actions – Ensure I am in bed by 10pm. Make sure I don't skip any meals. Keep doing my walks even if they are shorter. Make time to talk to friends.

Thinking – Check my thoughts for unhelpful negative thinking. Focus on the things I can control.

Feelings – Use my breathing to keep calm. Have a bath after work a couple of nights a week to relax. Pay attention to what my feelings are telling me.

SURVIVE

Which person or service will I contact if I am concerned about my mental health?

Name – Lifeline

Phone Number – 13 11 14

Figure 5: Sample Mental Health Fire Plan

Now it's your turn! Fill in the sheet below with the preparations, actions and emergency options for your own Mental Health Fire Plan.

MENTAL HEALTH
FIRE PLAN

PREPARE

What things will I do to promote and protect my mental health?

Actions –

_____

_____

_____

_____

_____

_____

Thinking –

_____

_____

_____

_____

_____

Feelings –

_____

_____

_____

_____

_____

ACT

Strategies I find helpful when life gets stressful:

Actions –

_____

_____

_____

_____

_____

_____

Thinking –

_____

_____

_____

_____

_____

_____

Feelings –

_____

_____

_____

_____

SURVIVE

Which person or service will I contact if I am concerned about my mental health?

Name - _____

_____

Phone Number/Contact Details - _____

_____

Happy successful life – thrive!

Now that you have your plan for good mental health and wellbeing, you will go on to live a happy and successful life – right?

Well, the fact is that life can be like a rollercoaster ride. There are times when you are riding high and elated; at other points you will drop suddenly or be thrown into a loop, and your heart will sink. Having good mental health and wellbeing doesn't mean you are happy all the time – it means that you know how to ride the rollercoaster.

We know that when the rollercoaster is slowly climbing up towards the summit, we can relax and take in the view. When it crests the top we know it's about to plummet and pick up speed fast, so we brace ourselves, pushing our body back into the seat. Some people will let out a scared-yet-thrilled scream when they start to drop, while others will have a grin plastered on their face. However you let out your feelings, the handy thing about a rollercoaster is that you know what's coming, and you've prepared yourself for it.

Good mental health and wellbeing enables us to manage the thoughts and emotions that arise within us at times of stress or disappointment so that we can keep going and try again, until we ride the excitement of success. A good ride is full of a range of experiences, and so is a happy and successful life.

....

The Mental Health Fire Plan you are making
for yourself based on what you have
read and learnt about in this book is your
strategy for riding life's rollercoaster.

....

But before I send you off into the wide world, there's one more thing to consider – and that's how you can create a ripple effect. Let's explore that next.

HOLIDAY! HOLIDAY! HOLIDAY!

Many years ago, a business leader came to see me because his struggles with stress were impacting his personal relationships. He was a highly driven man who clearly worked hard; he was very organised and focused, and had a clear business strategy. As we unpacked how he currently managed his stress, it became clear that he did in fact have a routine to do so – however, it was a somewhat risky one.

It turned out he would work long, hard long hours for around a year to eighteen months until he 'hit the wall', and then he would take an overseas holiday for a few weeks to completely disengage from work. He would return refreshed, and then the pattern would repeat itself. When I asked about the cost of this routine, he assured me that he was adept at finding very affordable holiday packages that were inexpensive but high-quality.

While the strategy seemed financially feasible, there were other costs to consider – the cost to his personal relationships, for one, given that when he was 'on' he was so busy working that there was much less time for social enjoyment. Also, I had to wonder how effective and productive he could be as he started to get run down before finally 'hitting the wall'. What if the moment when he absolutely needed to take his holiday coincided with a critical time in his business?

We began working on embedding daily mental health and wellbeing behaviours into his life: taking time to have breakfast with his family each morning; making sure to go for a daily run; engaging in leisure activities he enjoys; adjusting an unhelpful thought pattern such as, 'If I don't work hard all the time, I'm not good enough,' to 'If I look after myself, I can work well all the time.' By managing his mental health on a daily and weekly basis rather than waiting for that inevitable crash, he ensured that he remained consistently productive and performing at his best. In this new plan, holidays were now more proactive rather than a crisis response.

All this meant that he was now able to manage his business successfully without 'hitting the wall', and could take holidays at times that suited both his business and his family. His relationship with his family was more positive, as he was less irritable and snappy, and they were able to enjoy more time together as he had now made sure to build that time into his schedule.

CHAPTER 7

Leading others

Have you ever thrown a stone into a pond or lake and watched the ripples slowly expand across the water? The earthquake in the ocean near Tonga, in January 2022, created a massive global ripple effect. Rising nearly 39 kilometres into the sky, the volcanic eruption produced an ash cloud 260 kilometres wide. The shock wave was so massive it could be observed by satellites in space.

The waves of the ripple effect were recorded around the globe by seismometers. Metre-high waves hit the shores of Australia, New Zealand, Japan, the west coasts of North and South America, and even Alaska, which is over 9,000 kilometres away from the site of the quake. One event in one location impacted the world [28].

You could say that the COVID-19 pandemic is another example of a ripple effect. We live in such a mobile society these days, what with the availability of air travel and families being spread across the world, that when a new virus infected one city in China it quickly made its way around the globe, impacting people in every country on the planet.

The ripple effect of COVID-19 changed our daily lives in ways we could never have previously imagined. We wore masks when leaving our homes; we scanned entry into shops and venues that we visited; we kept our distance from others, and had to think twice about greeting people with a handshake or a hug.

A ripple effect can apply equally to peoples' influence. Look at leaders such as Mahatma Gandhi, Rosa Parks, Martin Luther King or Nelson Mandela. These were individuals who were facing down some of the most powerful forces in their society: the British Empire in India, racial inequality and the lack of civil rights in the United States, and the racist apartheid system of South Africa. They all ultimately dedicated their lives to the causes of freedom and equality by using peaceful means, offering forgiveness to their enemies – even as their enemies used violence against them. By never wavering in their dedication, they helped inspire thousands of others to move in the same direction, and bring about fundamental changes that had previously seemed impossible.

As a leader, you always want to have an impact. One of the greatest impacts you can have is to set an example of good mental health for your workforce. It starts with YOU.

....

Imagine the ripple effect we could have on the world if we led the way by showing others how we care for our own mental health and wellbeing.

....

It starts with you

As a leader in your organisation, you get to start the ripple effect. We have a responsibility to the people we employ, the customers to whom we provide services, and the community in which we live. Knowing this, perhaps you have already made efforts to put mental health supports in place for your workforce. You may have arranged presentations for your staff about how to look after one's mental health and wellbeing. Or, as a member of a leadership team, you could have been part of developing policies to manage mental health in the workplace.

But, even as you were doing these things, were you thinking about how you manage your mental health and wellbeing, and did you seek to make positive changes for yourself?

....

As a leader you will start a ripple effect in one way or another. How you live your life and look after your mental health and wellbeing will ripple through your workplace and community. What kind of ripple are you sending out?

....

You may genuinely be making efforts to help improve the mental health and wellbeing of those in and associated with your organisation, so how you think, feel and act about your own mental health will amplify those positive ripples you are already sending out. As leaders, it's easy for us to neglect ourselves even as we're seeking the best for the people who work for us: for instance, you may fully believe that people in your organisation who are struggling with their mental health should be given the proper support to address their wellbeing, but in your own case you are convinced that, given your role, you simply cannot take time out to care for yourself. But if the mental health and wellbeing of people in your organisation is truly important to you, then you need to lead by example and create that ripple effect.

Leaders are influential

I can't tell you how many times I have heard leaders say something along the lines of, 'I will worry about me later – there is work to be done, and I just need the mental health difficulties of my workforce addressed so that the organisation can function well.' But do you remember my own story back in Chapter 3, about when I was heading up the youth mental health team?

I thought I could help my team if I just worked harder, but the harder I worked, the more breaks I skipped, and the more hours I put in, so too did the team. No amount of me telling people they needed to take a lunch break, or advising them to leave on time tonight, truly inspired the team to care for their mental health. I had created the ripple through my behaviour, and it spread like a tsunami after an earthquake. Many of the people on my team ran themselves down into complete exhaustion, as did I.

There is power in understanding the ripple effect. What I choose to emanate from myself is the ripple that I create. As a leader, I want my people to know they are valued and important; I want them to know how to look after their mental health and wellbeing so they can live a full, purposeful and productive life. It all starts with *me* taking breaks, getting sleep, going for walks, having time out at the day spa, to become as efficient and effective as I can be when I am working.

....

If you want to know what kind of ripple effect you may be having in your organisation, take some time to observe how your workforce is thinking and feeling. Pay attention to the general and commonly accepted behaviours in the workplace.

....

You will note that I'm suggesting here that you observe workforce behaviours overall, rather than focusing on one or two individuals. As a leader you have influence, but each person is still unique, and some will be able to be influenced more than others. I have seen workplaces where the bulk of the staff are hard-working and skilled at their job, but there are one or two people whose main skill is disappearing when a difficult task needs to get done. Equally, there are workplaces where there is a general culture of low productivity, but which contains a couple of workhorses who effectively carry the team.

What key actions are you seeing in your workplace? What beliefs do your workforce hold about mental health and wellbeing? Is your workforce happy to be there, and are they engaged in the vision and goals of the organisation? These signs will tell you something about the influence you may be having as a leader.

Follow the Leader

Do you remember playing Follow the Leader as a child? Someone would be chosen as the leader, and the rest of us had to follow them and copy their actions. If the leader stood on one leg and rubbed their tummy, we all did the same. When the leader clapped their hands or stomped their feet three times or waved their hands over their head, so did we. Ah, simpler days!

Being all grown up and trying to lead a team isn't quite like playing Follow the Leader. In the game, someone not following the leader was declared 'out' – I guess that's roughly similar to someone being terminated from a position, but the decision to end someone's job isn't as automatic as that (and it shouldn't be, either!). Even though we're not playing kids' games in our workplace, we need to remember that most people in an organisation *do* watch and copy their leader to some extent. If the leader skips lunch breaks, works long hours, and gets overtired and run down, chances are there will be staff who do the same.

The good news, though, is that people will also watch and copy a leader who is positive, motivated, enthusiastic and has a clear plan. So here are a few simple steps you can put in place to have a positive influence on your workforce.

1. Set the example

In the game of Follow the Leader, the leader does the action first so the others can mimic and follow. The leader doesn't say 'clap your hands' and then stand back, waiting for the others to do as they are told; instead, the leader claps three times and pauses to indicate to the others to do the same. The leader starts by *setting* the example to follow – not ordering people, but personally *showing* the action.

If you as a leader are following your Mental Health Fire Plan, which includes things like working reasonable hours, taking regular breaks to eat lunch or go for a short walk, and sipping a peppermint tea (or your soothing beverage of choice!) during a long tough meeting and, as a result, are no longer exhausted all the time, less moody or grumpy, not snapping at people in meetings, and happy and productive, people will see that it is okay for them to do the things necessary to look after their mental health and wellbeing. By setting the example yourself, you have given your workforce permission to follow.

I have worked in teams where the manager makes a point of taking a lunch break, and I see the staff doing the same. They don't even consider skipping lunch, as it is the workplace practice, from the leader down, to take a break to eat. Some managers I have worked with go for a walk during their break, and I've then noticed some of their staff do the same. People are willing to follow the example of their leader.

....

Ask yourself – what example am I
setting for others to follow?

....

2. Create the space

It is all well and good for us as leaders to be looking after our own mental health and wellbeing by taking breaks, ensuring we get home on time and, by doing so, setting a great example to follow.

However, if we haven't thoughtfully set up the work environment and expectations, and communicated those to our staff, there might not be the time or space available to care for their mental health and wellbeing, even though we have given permission and set the tone.

It is not reasonable for you as the CEO, manager or leader to make time in your schedule for a game of golf or a monthly massage if your employees are rostered so heavily that they don't have a chance to look after themselves as well.

This is remarkably common. In many workplaces there is more work to do than hours in the day. We need to use our leadership skills wisely, manage our stress from the pressure of demands, keep our thinking brain on so we can use our higher-level problem-solving abilities, and set priorities and workflow management that is effective, efficient, and reasonable for all our staff. When we do this, it enables everyone to take the breaks they need for lunch, for a day off, or for regular annual leave.

....

Ask yourself – am I creating a space and opportunity for everyone in my workplace to be able to look after their mental health?

....

3. Allow individuality

Lastly, we need to remember that each person is unique: we all have our likes and dislikes, our preferences and our habits. As I mentioned earlier, I prefer to do my thinking work in the morning when my brain is fresh, but other people don't get going until later in the day – so when my brain is powering down come evening, their brain is starting to fire on all cylinders. There are some people who work best while listening to music, but others need the office to be completely quiet to be able to think. I like to work at a seated desk, but I've also worked with colleagues who prefer a standing desk.

When it comes to mental health and wellbeing strategies, we need to understand the broad principles of what is truly effective, but also allow our staff flexibility in how they apply them.

....

Ask yourself – do you allow flexibility and individuality in the workplace for staff to care for their mental health in the ways that work best for them?

....

Remember, you can show your employees the way to care for their mental health by leading by example and creating the space and time for them to engage in their mental health activities, but without allowing them the freedom to choose those activities that work best for them it can all come to naught. Each person's Mental Health Fire Plan will look different, and that's why, collectively, they will work to make a happier and more productive workforce.

We all succeed

When a CEO or senior leader makes a decision, demonstrates an action and lives out a vision, it starts a ripple. That ripple could be one that spreads positive mental health and wellbeing throughout an entire organisation.

Mental health difficulties cost the global economy US$1 trillion per year in lost productivity, according to WHO estimates. But statistics also show that, for every US$1 put into scaled-up treatment for common mental disorders, there is a return of US$4 in improved health and productivity [4].

Why wait until someone is mentally unwell and needs urgent treatment? It is far more cost-effective to *prevent* people becoming stressed, burned out, depressed and anxious. When we as leaders seek to positively influence our workplace by demonstrating the benefits of good mental health and wellbeing, we can contribute to the creation of a mentally healthy and fit workforce overall, filled with happy and productive employees who are performing at their best every day.

....

When we as leaders succeed, everyone can succeed.
When we take the time to value and care for our mental health and wellbeing, so will those in our circle of influence.

....

RIPPLE EFFECT

Can you think of a leader you know or have worked with whom you admire? What are the characteristics or attributes that drew you to that person?

In my case, the leaders I most admire have a calmness about them. They are hard-working and highly intelligent, but above all they are level-headed. I was observing a leader in their workplace recently who had to make a presentation. I knew they were stressed, as we had spoken before the session and they had informed me that the technology wasn't working properly, which had forced them to change their whole plan for the presentation.

I felt they held themselves well, delivering their material articulately and with clarity. After the session I commended them on a job well done, only for them to explain just how many things had not gone to plan. I commented that because they had been able to stay calm even while under stress, they had been able to troubleshoot as they went along without anyone noticing.

This leader has a work–life balance that suits them. They ensure they are well-rested, they keep active, and they stay connected with trusted and supportive friends. They know how to breathe and remain calm so they can think strategically. They have a plan to maintain good mental health, and they follow it.

Even better, others around them notice and follow: their colleagues see how they manage their mental health, and then they do likewise. This is the ripple effect. And it starts with you living out the values and principles that you want to see not only in your own life, but also in your workplace and community.

Conclusion

On our fifth day on the mountain, I woke to the sound of our guide calling my name. Pulling on my thermal layers and hiking boots, I headed to the dining tent to join the rest of our group. While I didn't feel hungry, I knew I had to keep slowly swallowing one mouthful of warm porridge at a time. I checked that my backpack had all I needed: water, headtorch, medical supplies, snacks.

At midnight, we started to climb. Our group walked in single file, one step at a time, through the darkness. Words of encouragement came from our guides and others in the group. At times when I felt overwhelmed, I would coach myself, saying in my head 'right foot then left foot ...'

As dawn broke, we sat and rested with a hot cup of tea as we watched the sun begin to rise. I stood up from the rock where I was sitting, pulled my backpack on, and kept climbing. I was now moving at a glacial speed in a slow shuffle, no longer lifting my feet.

Finally, there it was – the summit. I had made it. I stood with our group for a photo in front of the wooden sign. I was standing 5,895 metres above sea level on the second-tallest mountain in the world. I had just summitted Mount Kilimanjaro.

I am not a sporty person. Physical challenges are not my forte. Our head guide told me it was my mental strength that got me to the top. There were people who set out to climb Kilimanjaro who are much fitter than me, but who have not made the top. Climbing a mountain is as much about your mental health as it is your physical health.

....

Leading an organisation, starting a business, or being a CEO is much like climbing a mountain – you need to have good mental health and wellbeing to be able to reach the summit.

....

Leadership requires stamina. The climb is long and often uphill, and if you don't rest regularly, you won't be able to keep going. If you skip meals and are not fuelling your body, you will struggle to keep working. When you feel overwhelmed, you need to be able to harness your mind and focus on your goal.

Just as we can take steps to have good physical health, we can do the same for our mental health.

Don't leave your mental health to chance. Have a plan. Be prepared. Know what to do when you are under stress or pressure. Seek extra help if you need it. Your mental health and wellbeing is a good investment. Your ripple effect could change not only your own productivity and performance, but also that of your whole workforce.

All it takes is to put one foot in front of the other.

I would never ask a client to do something I was not prepared to do myself (and probably already have done). I have had to learn the same lessons as those I'm teaching. I have days where I succeed, but I also have days where I am overwhelmed and must work hard on my mental health.

Again, all it takes is one simple step – one foot in front of the other.

The key to good mental health and wellbeing is doing something about it. So, start putting into practice what you have learned from this book.

It might feel uncomfortable when you start, and it will be hard work. But I promise you, you will eventually look down from the top and know it was all worth it.

Julie

Connect With Me

I love that you valued your own mental health enough to read this book!

If you are like me, you have probably made some changes already based on the ideas you have encountered here. However, sometimes we need a little extra help to make things happen.

This book is in your hands because I put in the hard yards to get it written, but it took the right book coach and editor to get my plan in place and give me the support required to get it over the line.

I walked every step to get to the top of Mount Kilimanjaro, but it was the amazing guides that set the pace and provided the encouragement I needed to keep going and complete the climb.

If you would like some extra support or help to become a mentally fit leader, go to **julierowse.com.au** to connect with me!

MENTAL HEALTH
FIRE PLAN

Sources

[1] Zubin, J., & Spring, B. (1977). Vulnerability: A new view of schizophrenia. *Journal of Abnormal Psychology*, 86(2), 103–126. https://doi.org/10.1037/0021-843X.86.2.103

[2] Deutsch, S. (2021). "I had three CEOs on the phone to me crying": Leaders' mental health needs urgent attention. *HRM*. https://www.hrmonline.com.au/mental-health/three-of-my-ceos-were-on-the-phone-to-me-crying-leaders-mental-health-needs-urgent-attention/

[3] Editorial team (2021). Is there mental health support for your CEOs? *Horton International*. https://www.hortoninternational.com/news/is-there-mental-health-support-for-your-ceos

[4] World Health Organisation. (2022). Mental health in the workplace. https://www.who.int/teams/mental-health-and-substance-use/promotion-prevention/mental-health-in-the-workplace

[5] Australian Government Productivity Commission. (2020). Mental health report. https://www.pc.gov.au/inquiries/completed/mental-health#report

[6] Parke, C. (2019). Once burned out, twice shy: The unaffordable cost of work-related stress. https://www.openaccessgovernment.org/cost-of-work-related-stress/71555/#:~:text=Work%2Drelated%20stress%20and%20mental,%C2%A39%20billion%20a%20year

[7] Brearley, B. (2019). Why good mental health is a leader's best friend. *Thoughtful Leader*. https://www.thoughtfulleader.com/why-good-mental-health-is-a-leaders-best-friend/#:~:text=Leaders%20Need%20Good%20Mental%20Health%20to%20Show%20Empathy&text=When%20you%20genuinely%20care%20about,problems%20than%20ofocus%20oon%20oothers

[8] Brooker, D. (2019). Just because you're a high achiever doesn't mean mental health is not for you. *Forbes*. https://www.forbes.com/sites/daniellebrooker/2019/05/28/just-because-youre-a-high-achiever-doesnt-mean-mental-health-is-not-for-you/?sh=182f2701798b

[9] Bupa Newsroom. (2018). Two thirds of business leaders have suffered from mental health conditions. https://www.bupa.com/newsroom/news/business-leaders-mental-health-study

[10] Seppälä, E. & Cameron, K. (2015). Proof that positive work cultures are more productive. *Harvard Business Review*. https://hbr.org/2015/12/proof-that-positive-work-cultures-are-more-productive

[11] Anon. (2021). Sleep and mental health. *Harvard Health Publishing: Harvard Medical School.* https://www.health.harvard.edu/newsletter_article/sleep-and-mental-health

[12] Brennan,D. (2021). What to know about vitamins and mental health. *WebMD.* https://www.webmd.com/vitamins-and-supplements/what-to-know-about-vitamins-and-mental-health#:~:text=A%20diet%20that%20includes%20vitamin,have%20been%20linked%20to%20depression

[13] Sharma, A., Madaan, V., & Petty, F. D. (2006). Exercise for mental health. *Primary Care Companion to the Journal of Clinical Psychiatry, 8*(2), 106. https://doi.org/10.4088/pcc.v08n0208a

[14] WebMD. (2021) Psychological benefits of routines. https://www.webmd.com/mental-health/psychological-benefits-of-routine

[15] Truong, K. (2018) Here's why venting about stress feels so good. *Wellness.* https://www.refinery29.com/en-us/venting-talking-to-someone-benefits#:~:text=Eva%20Stubits%2C%20PhD%2C%20a%20Houston,process%20them%2C%22%20she%20says

[16] Ward, F. (2022). The Queen's sleep routine is so simple but so effective, and she apparently sticks to it every single night. *Glamour.* https://www.glamourmagazine.co.uk/article/the-queen-sleep-routine#:~:text=Apparently%2C%20Her%20Majesty%20always%20goes,Sounds%20reasonable%20to%20us.&text=It's%20so%20simple

[17] Pratt, E. (2020). Negative thinking can harm your brain and increase your dementia risk. *Health News.* https://www.healthline.com/health-news/negative-thinking-can-harm-brain-increase-dementia-risk

[18] Harvard Medical School Blog. (2021). Giving thanks can make you happier. *Harvard Health Publishing.* https:// .health.harvard.edu/healthbeat/giving-thanks-can-make-you-happier

[19] Wizarding World Digital. (2018). 500 million Harry Potter books have now been sold worldwide. *Wizarding World.* https://www.wizardingworld.com/news/500-million-harry-potter-books-have-now-been-sold-worldwide

[20] Hall, D. (2022) JK Rowling turned down by 12 publishers before finding success with Harry Potter books. *Rise up eight.org Fall Down Seven Times, Rise Up Eight.* https://riseupeight.org/jk-rowling-harry-potter-books/

[21] Current, R. (2022). The road to presidency. *Britannica.* https://www.britannica.com/biography/Abraham-Lincoln/The-road-to-presidency

[22] Gillard, J. (2017). The stigma around mental health nearly cost Australia its greatest leader. *Guardian.* https://www.theguardian.com/commentisfree/2017/jun/29/julia-gillard-the-stigma-around-mental-health-nearly-cost-australia-its-greatest-leader

[23] Ghaemi, N. (2015). Winston Churchill and his 'black dog' of greatness. *The Conversation.* https://theconversation.com/winston-churchill-and-his-black-dog-of-greatness-36570

[24] Hawkins, D. (2020). Tough times call for emotionally intelligent CEOs. *Forbes Coaches Council.* https://www.forbes.com/sites/forbescoachescouncil/2020/11/09/tough-times-call-for-emotionally-intelligent-ceos/?sh=37ac6f1d5121

[25] Australian Institute of Health & Welfare (AIHW) (2020). Mental health. *AIHW online.* https://www.aihw.gov.au/reports/australias-health/mental-health

[26] World Health Organisation (2021). Depression. https://www.who.int/news-room/fact-sheets/detail/depression

[27] Beyond Blue. (2022). Statistics. https://www.beyondblue.org.au/media/statistics

[28] Ramesh, S. (2022). Volcanic eruption on tiny Tonga shook the world: What we know about the causes and impact so far. *The Print.* https://theprint.in/science/volcanic-eruption-on-tiny-tonga-shook-the-world-what-we-know-about-the-causes-and-impact-so-far/809422/